SO YOU WANT TO BE A
YOUTUBER?

SO YOU WANT TO BE A
YOUTUBER?

*The Secrets of How to Turn Your Passion
Into a Viable Career on YouTube*

By SilentcOre
Over 100 million YouTube views!

ISBN: 9781071106457

Cover designed by Ojedokun Daniel Olusegun.

Proof read by Stuart Harper.

This book is not authorised or endorsed by YouTube, Google or any other person or entity owning or controlling rights in the YouTube name, trademark or copyright.

The suggestions within this book are based on my experience with YouTube and other creators. They are not a guarantee for success and every channel may have different results.

First Edition 2019

www.silentcOre.com

TABLE OF CONTENTS

INTRODUCTION

YouTube can offer so many unique opportunities: Being a part of passionate communities with similar interests; Building skills to open up new career paths; Creating a business by monetising your passion points.

This book aims to help aspiring creators turn a passion into a living on YouTube. I will take you through the fundamentals of creating a channel, building a brand and growing an audience - to the more advanced strategies of converting viewers into fans, collaborating with brands, earning sponsorships and generating a passive income on YouTube.

It is never too late to get started, and throughout this book I will show you why.

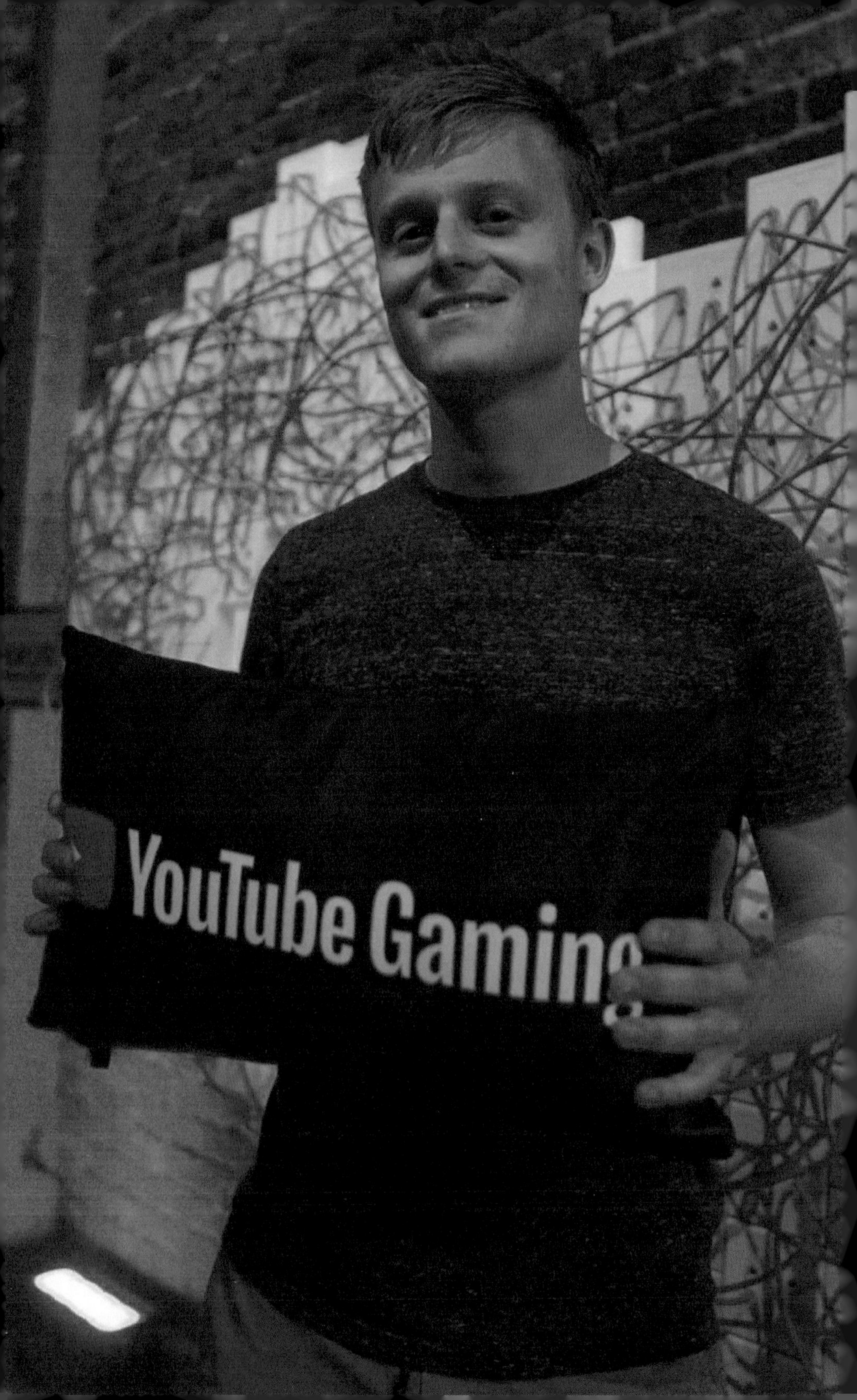
YouTube Gamin

ABOUT THE AUTHOR

As an early adopter of YouTube I have had the incredible opportunity to experience the YouTube platform throughout its major algorithm changes as it has been adopted around the world into a common household name.

Since launching my channel in 2007 I have accumulated over 100 million video views and 350,000 YouTube Subscribers. Since then I have been able to collaborate with major international brands, set multiple Guinness World Records and speak at panels sharing my experience on the platform.

In 2017 I became the first official YouTube Ambassador in Scotland and was invited to host official YouTube Creator events around the United Kingdom.

Currently I am based in Toronto, Canada and connect social media influencers with paid brand deals.

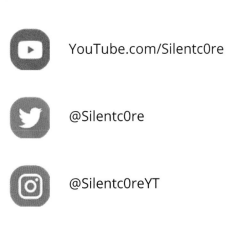 YouTube.com/Silentc0re

@Silentc0re

@Silentc0reYT

 Facebook.com/Silentc0re

"JUST START UPLOADING"

The biggest barrier to becoming successful on YouTube, is simply starting. This is where most people get caught up - and end up taking no action at all.

Did you know Pewdiepie - currently the most subscribed individual on YouTube - uploaded over 100 videos just to reach 2,500 subscribers?

I am going to assume since you have purchased this book (or illegally downloaded it!), that you are passionate enough to invest your own time and resources into becoming a YouTuber, the next step is to pull the trigger.

Excuses only prevent us from following our dreams.

The first step is to **just start uploading**!

THE 5 FAMOUS EXCUSES

Here are some of the most common reasons why people procrastinate about starting a YouTube channel, and I will carefully explain exactly why each one is completely irrelevant.

1. "IT IS TOO LATE TO START A CHANNEL"

There is no denying there is considerably more competition on the YouTube platform than when I started back in 2007.

However, this has a similar lining as YouTube today has a much bigger viewer audience than it did when I started. YouTube now has over 1.9 billion monthly viewers - and that is just the users logged in! Not to mention there are also far greater opportunities available today with official YouTube creator events, conferences, networking summits and an increasing number of brands looking to invest large marketing budgets in online influencers.

Besides - getting in early also does not guarantee any success. This is like music producers justifying not making music as there are already too many good artists playing on the radio, or movie directors deciding not to launch a film because there are already too many films out there.

2. "I DON'T HAVE THE TIME"

Generally, the older we get, the more commitments and responsibilities we have. However, everyone has the same amount of time in the day. It is what we do with that time that counts.

Ask yourself how many times you have checked your phone today? How many hours have you watched TV or Netflix this week? Give priority to actions that will benefit you in the long-term and fit in the recreational activities around it.

My personal biggest weakness is consuming too many YouTube videos and not creating my own! I try to set aside 30 minutes per day to watch videos, and then assign the rest of the day to my own work.

3. "I DO NOT HAVE ENOUGH MONEY OR THE RIGHT EQUIPMENT"

It is a common misconception that you must have the best equipment to make it on YouTube. My first microphone was a cheap £10 headset that I recorded on my parent's desktop computer. Modern smartphones are able to record in HD quality, meaning most people already have enough equipment to get started.

As your channel grows, you can invest in a better microphone, camera or editing software. When your friends and family ask what you want for your birthday or Christmas - ask them for presents that will help you improve the quality of your videos. For a complete list of my recommended equipment, see page 127.

4. "I DO NOT HAVE THE RIGHT CONNECTIONS"

From the outside it might seem like all successful YouTubers know each other. And without being in their inner circle - you have no chance of succeeding.

While being friends with already established influencers can help kick-start a channel, the vast majority of creators do *not* have this privilege. There are thousands of YouTube creators out there just like you who are also looking for collaborations. The good news is that social media allows us to reach almost anyone, so making connections is easier than ever before.

5. "I AM EMBARRASSED TO FAIL"

No one wants to publically fail at something. If you are still at high school, this point may be particularly relevant.

The people who try to bring you down will be the ones too scared to try themselves. Find support from people who respect you for trying to succeed and who will motivate you to continue. Try encouraging a few friends or classmates into creating channels with you and support each other.

ESTABLISHING A CHANNEL BRAND

You want to give your YouTube channel the best possible chance to succeed on the platform. In this chapter I will take you through all of the essential aspects of creating, branding and establishing a memorable channel.

Each chapter in this book starts with a summary, outing the major themes covered in each chapter. At the end of each chapter you will find a checklist, think of this as a list of actionable points to implement to your own YouTube channel.

INCLUDED IN CHAPTER 1

☑ *Finding a content niche on YouTube*

☑ *Assess your content category*

☑ *Define your Mission Statement*

☑ *Creating a Brand*

FINDING A CONTENT NICHE

If there was only *one* tip I could give an aspiring creator, it would be to locate the right niche to create content.

It is worth considering - whatever you are interested in - whether there are going to be other people out there with the same interests. Take whatever you are passionate about - whether it is travel, sports, cooking, games or movies - and find your niche within that category. Start thinking of your channel as a community of people that are interested in your subject.

ThePrenti is a creator from Scotland and found a niche on YouTube in drink crafting. As a bartender and barista by profession, he uses his passion, knowledge and experience to create cocktails. He also has a series where he challenges himself to drink beverages in under a minute, however I wouldn't recommend this for obvious reasons!

It's a common misconception to think *'Gaming is a huge audience, so I'll make gaming videos for everyone that's interested in games'*. Now while gaming *is* currently the largest category on YouTube - that doesn't necessarily mean creating generalised gaming videos is your best chance at making it big. Quite the opposite actually. If you take a look at most large creators in the gaming vertical, it is more than likely they will have initially established themselves in a niche market. Once you have an already established viewer-base, it is much easier for you to expand into a wider genre.

Creating niche content also compliments YouTube's algorithm. By growing a niche following, you are fostering a more dedicated community of viewers who will engage more with your content, rather than posting generalised content that will only resonate with some of your audience.

Here are a few examples of Niche content:

- You are passionate about a sport such as dog agility - this is an excellent niche you can create content around.

- You are a keen chef and want to start a general cooking channel - start with a speciality and focus on it e.g. desserts, Indian cuisines.

- One of your hobbies is making cocktails - there could be room for a go-to channel for drink crafting.

- Instead of creating a 'let's play' gaming channel - find a specific game franchise or sub-genre you are most interested in e.g. *Pokémon* games, *Nintendo* products or *Assassin's Creed*.

ASSESS YOUR CONTENT CATEGORY

Every channel on YouTube can be associated with a content category. This allows viewers to easily find content they want to watch within that category as well as allowing advertisers to reach their target audience. Content categories can include Auto, Beauty, Comedy, Entertainment, Food, Gaming, Music, News, Animals, Science, Sports and Travel.

Of course, many channels post content that fits into multiple categories. However, the bulk of your content should be focused within **one** major content category to help build focus, momentum and relevancy with your target audience. Viewers can be put off by a channel if it appears too messy with too many content categories.

While considering your channel's niche, it is also important to assess the landscape in your chosen content category. This will help you understand who your competition is, what similar channels are doing, who your target audience is, what they respond well to, and what potential value you can add to your category.

Here are a few examples of questions to critique a potential category.

Who are the largest creators and
what specifically are they known for?

- How many top channels are in your chosen category? Is there one large channel dominating, or multiple medium sized channels?

- Is the channel regularly working with brands for paid product placement or sponsorships? Are the brands specifically related to your content category?

- How frequent is their upload schedule? Are they maintaining regular viewership on every video and reaching new subscribers?

Who is the target audience within this category?

- Evaluate the audience watching within your category - how old are they, where are they geographically located, gender etc.

- How engaged are the audience with the content? Check the comment section on the videos to evaluate if the audience sentiment is positive. What videos do they enjoy most or do not enjoy?

- Identify any viral videos? Check the videos uploaded from previous months - have any performed exceptionally well within your category? Was it extremely sharable or had it an attractive thumbnail to drive viewership?

What is the category missing?

- How high is the production value? Are they recording with a webcam or more professional camera equipment? Could the videos be more concisely edited?

- Regularly uploading? Are they satisfying their audience with enough content?

- Are they showing their personality enough? If the channels are overly focused on the content and not themselves - could there be room for more personality based content?

DEFINE YOUR MISSION STATEMENT

If you are not sure of the direction you are taking your YouTube channel in, any potential new viewers will also be unsure. There is nothing more off putting to viewers than a channel that does not have an identity. Give your channel a purpose - what is your channel aiming to achieve?

Clearly define your mission statement, *who* are your videos for and *what* is the value to your target audience. By openly communicating this, you are setting viewer expectations and giving your channel a value proposition by offering a reason for viewers to Subscribe.

Here are a few examples of strong mission statements:

- **CakesByChoppA:** A channel dedicated to showing step-by-step how to easily make and decorate a cake for any occasion.

- **SwitchForce:** All of the latest News and Updates for the Nintendo Switch gaming console.

- **Daily Bumps:** Each video is a new fun family activity. Although the activities in each video are different the channel mission statement remains the same with the consistent family appearances.

- **HumbleMechanic:** This channel is run by a certified technician who demonstrates DIY car maintenance, vehicle modifications and reviews tools and equipment used by mechanics.

CREATING A BRAND

Even when first starting your channel you should be thinking and treating it, as a brand. Everything from your channel name, your channel banner, to your video content makes up your brand. Even you! These components should all be consistent in painting the picture of your brand and reinforcing your mission statement.

Channel Name

Your channel name should ideally represent your brand. This could be your real name, an alias you use online, or a name that tributes your content.

It is a good idea to make sure that your channel name does not already exist to save yourself some potential future complications. So do a quick search on YouTube to make sure there will not be any conflicts with other established creators.

Dragon City Fan is a YouTube channel dedicated to the mobile game 'Dragon City'. Using the game name within his channel name, has helped him rank within the first few results on YouTube when making a search query for the game's name "Dragon City". With so much content covering the video game, his fan channel even ranks higher than the official Dragon City YouTube channel!

Dragon City Fan ✔
291,263 subscribers • 4,628 videos
Dragon City Fan is a channel provides information of the facebook & mobile game ... !! **Dragon City**: Game news & update, ...

Channel names can also be a powerful Search Engine Optimisation (SEO) tool to have your channel rank higher in your content category. Consider what search terms and phrases viewers may be searching for around your chosen content category - can you integrate this into your channel name?

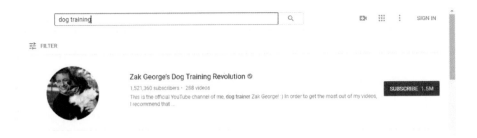

If you search *'Dog Training'* on YouTube, the first result is a channel called *'Zak George's Dog Training Revolution'.* This is a fantastic way to get your channel in front of the audience that are actually looking for the type of content that you are making.

Custom Channel URL

Once you have decided on your channel name, you can set up a custom URL for your YouTube channel. It will appear as *youtube.com/ yourcustomurl.* This is highly recommended, as it gives your channel an easy to remember web address for visitors to your page. You should choose a custom URL that is easy to remember and matches your channel name.

To claim a custom URL in the channel settings section you must meet the following eligibility requirements:

- 100 Subscribers
- Uploaded a custom channel banner and icon
- Channel that is at least 30 days old

To maintain consistency across platforms, it is also a good idea to go ahead and register the same name on all major social media platforms (Facebook, Twitter, Instagram etc). Even if you do not initially plan on using them all - I can confidently say from experience it is much easier to register them for yourself than try to claim them back from someone else.

Additionally, registering the same name as a domain (such as *yourchannelurl.com*) is a worthwhile investment. Again, it is much easier to do this initially yourself, rather than try to pry it back from someone else who has already registered it. When a company registered my YouTube username as a domain, they demanded several thousand dollars to reclaim it! Thankfully after a few years they released it and I was able to register it within my own name. Registering your own domain is a small price to pay to save any future complications. If you do not have your own website or blog you can simply make the domain redirect straight to your YouTube channel page.

Channel Icon

Your channel avatar or icon is visible on YouTube and all Google products. This should look good in small and larger sizes as it will be displayed in different places. The channel icon is visible on your channel's homepage, the video watch page, and also if your channel is linked within a video using an end card (more about that in Chapter 2).

It can also be beneficial to have a channel avatar or logo professionally made to better represent your brand. Can a viewer tell what kind of content you make from your icon or logo alone?

Australian Creator SimpleCookingChannel, uses a crafty channel icon to represent his brand. It features his signature chef hat that he wears within his cooking videos and you can clearly see what his channel is all about from his icon alone.

Channel Banner

Your channel's banner is a huge real estate to impress viewers that visit your channel page. Use this space to reinforce your branding, personality and what you are offering on YouTube. You could also include your upload schedule within the banner to let your viewers know when they should check back.

You should regularly check YouTube's recommended banner sizes as they can change with a major UI (user interface) update. Your banner will display at different sizes depending on the platform your viewers are using (such as a mobile, TV, game console, tablet etc). More than 50% of YouTube views come from mobile devices, so be sure to check your branding is still clear and no text is not cut off on any of the devices with smaller banners.

Clean my space uses a simple, yet effective banner. From the banner alone, you can see this is a cleaning channel, which uploads on a weekly basis. It also features Melissa Maker who appears in all the content to reinforce their branding.

Channel Description

You can include up to 1,000 characters in your channel description, so include: a short bio about your channel, who you are, what kinds of content you post and any other relevant information, such as your upload schedule.

A segment of your channel description will be visible in search results before viewers have clicked on your channel so this is another opportunity to include searchable keywords to help viewers discover your channel. Be sure to include the most important information at the start of the channel description to make the most of this space.

It can also be helpful to include links to your other social media platforms and include a business email address in this section. If any potential brands or advertisers visit your channel, you want to make it easy for them to find and contact you.

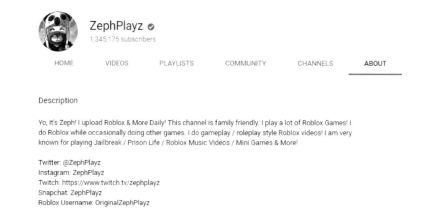

Roblox YouTuber 'ZephPlayz' starts his channel description by making it clear what his channel offers - daily Roblox videos. He also uses the word "Roblox" 6 times throughout the channel description to increase the searchability of his channel for search engine optimisation (SEO).

Channel Trailer

A channel trailer is the perfect way to introduce new viewers to your channel. If you do not have one, you **need** one. Simply featuring a recent video on your channel is unlikely to be the best way to represent your content as a whole. Instead think about what unique aspects your channel and personality offer and what would make potential viewers opt-in to subscribe and watch more of your content.

Take the time to produce a high quality trailer to give first time viewers the best possible impression of your channel. Do not try to 'wing' a trailer in one take. Scripting and planning exactly what you will say and showcasing your channel in a compact video is vital. Including a quirk to your trailer can also leave a lasting impression - if you are a comedy channel, include a joke!

- The ideal channel trailer should be around **1-2 minutes in length** and hook viewers within the first few seconds.

- Start off by **introducing** *who* you are and *what* your channel provides in a nutshell.

- Assume the viewers have never heard of you and tell them **why they should subscribe**.

- Finish with a **call to action** telling viewers to subscribe or watch more videos.

CHAPTER 1 CHECKLIST

Use this checklist to confirm you have taken all
the essential steps covered in this chapter:

☐ *Find a niche on the platform*

☐ *Define a mission statement*

☐ *Create a channel name that represents your brand*

☐ *Set up a custom channel URL that is easy for viewers
to remember*

☐ *Use memorable branding*

☐ *Create a custom channel trailer*

OPTIMISING YOUR CHANNEL

According to Google, over 400 hours of video content is uploaded to YouTube every single minute. That is 65 years of video per day!

With so much noise, it is imperative that you understand how YouTube's search and discovery algorithm works in order to further optimise your channel and videos to allow as many potential viewers as possible to find you.

INCLUDED IN CHAPTER 2

- ☑ *The YouTube algorithm*

- ☑ *Watch Time*

- ☑ *How to increase Watch Time and views*

- ☑ *Channel strategy and boosting discovery*

- ☑ *Translations*

THE YOUTUBE ALGORITHM

To understand how to get more views on YouTube, you first need to understand what qualities will encourage the YouTube algorithm promote your video. Of course no one knows the exact algorithm or formula, or else our videos would always be on the homepage getting millions of views! But, we can analyse what qualities YouTube looks for in a video to promote it.

The YouTube algorithm is a real-time feedback system that caters for each viewer differently. YouTube wants to encourage viewers to come back to YouTube time and time again, so YouTube presents them with videos that they think best fit what the viewer wants to watch. YouTube have stated that their recommendations are derived from over 80 billion pieces of information - extracted every day from the way viewers themselves interact with YouTube.

The videos served to viewers vary on the following factors:

- How much time they spend watching content

- What videos they watch or do not watch

- Their history of video likes and dislikes

- If they have marked any videos as *'not interested'*

The good news is that YouTube does not favour certain kinds of content, so, rest assured, whatever kind of videos you are making (sports, cooking, gaming etc) YouTube will continue to serve content that is relevant to your users.

WATCH TIME

With so much content being uploaded to YouTube, the YouTube algorithm needs a way to qualify and rank videos to make sure only the most relevant results are recommended and suggested to potential new viewers.

Before 2012, it was simply the number of views that drove discovery on the YouTube platform. So videos that accumulated high view counts would be deemed as worthy content and thus promoted on YouTube - further increasing the view count. However this system had some unintentional drawbacks - videos that were clickbait or had misleading thumbnails could game the system by increasing the video view count, even if the viewers did not stick around long enough to watch the entire video.

This all changed with the introduction of **Watch Time**. The number one ranking factor for YouTube today is Watch Time. Watch Time is defined by YouTube as *"The amount of time, in aggregate, that your viewers are watching your video"*. So essentially, the algorithm favours content that leads to your viewers watching more videos and increasing the length of time they spend watching YouTube. This allows YouTube to promote higher quality content that viewers want to watch, rather than a title and thumbnail that drives most clicks.

By creating great content that engages viewers to stick around and watch more, this will increase the Watch Time on your channel and thus increase the likelihood of YouTube promoting your videos.

Be aware the following can reduce your channel's Watch Time and make your videos less likely to appear in search results and recommended:

- **Clickbait:** Misleading or overly sensational video titles and thumbnails.

- **Inefficient editing:** Long or boring segments can cause viewers to skip ahead or leave the video completely.

- **Driving off-site:** If your viewers are leaving the YouTube platform entirely after watching your video, this can have a negative effect on your channel's overall Watch Time.

In Chapter 4 I will show you how to review your Watch Time analytics to evaluate your overall channel health.

HOW TO INCREASE WATCH TIME AND VIEWS ON YOUTUBE

To increase your channel's Watch Time, you first need to start accumulating views. To answer the million dollar question, *"how can I get more views on YouTube?"*, we first need to understand where views come from.

Views come from 7 main sources:

- Search Results
- Recommended Videos
- Home Page
- Trending
- Subscriptions
- Notifications
- External Sources

Search Results

YouTube is the 2nd largest search engine in the world, under Google. Utilising the users already searching for a specific kind of content can be a powerful source of views, especially if your channel is new.

Consider what people are actively searching for around your topic of choice and tap into these potential viewers. You can also catch traffic from relevant occasions - such as major events, holidays or trending topics. Fidget Spinners for example became a craze in 2017, offering a huge opportunity for channels to capitalise on the search interest on this topic. *Dude Perfect*, a channel known for trick-shot compilations created an episode during this time titled *"Fidget Spinner Trick Shots"* that now has nearly 100 million views making it one of the most viewed videos on their channel.

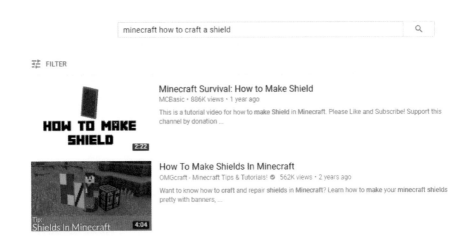

If you are integrating a popular event or holiday theme into a video, such as *Valentine's Day*, it is best published live *before* the event happens for maximum impact. A video covering a yearly holiday is unlikely to accumulate views all year round, but it will gain traction over the holiday period for which it is most relevant.

One of my favourite tools for analysing trends is Google's own *Google Trends Explore* (https://trends.google.com). This tool shows how frequently a given search term or query is entered into Google's search engine over a given period of time. You can enter multiple keywords and compare the historical search volumes.

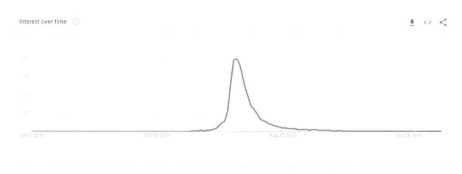

This graph shows the worldwide search interest over time for "Fidget Spinners". Notice the huge spike in search volume in May 2017.

This tool also offers the ability to breakdown the interest by country or even sub-region.

New Zealand and the United States had the highest proportion of queries for Fidget Spinners!

Another feature of Google Trends is to display topics and search phrases related to your search term. Related topics and queries are also highly useful for optimising your video as you can see what users searching for your term also searched for. If relevant, consider integrating these popular topics and search queries into your video's title, description and tags.

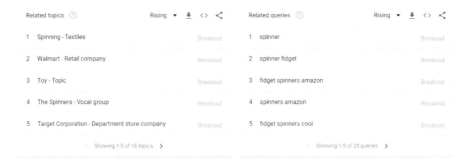

Users searching for "Fidget Spinners" also searched for the following related topics.

My favourite feature of Google Trends is being able to compare the search volumes for two different words or phrases. Here you can see the search volumes and thus the relative interest for two yearly celebrations, Valentine's Day and Saint Patrick's Day.

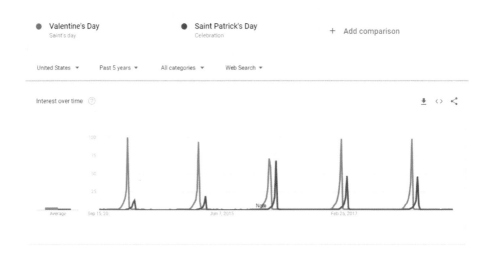

Creating content around recurring trends may give your content a longer-term uplift rather than a single spike

Create Evergreen Content

While creating content around popular trends can drive a big spike in viewers, evergreen content is important for long-term growth. Evergreen content is content that is always of interest to viewers and has a long shelf life. If your videos will not be relevant or shared in 6 months' time, they are not evergreen.

Try choosing a 'base' keyword and cycle through the alphabet to find even more content ideas!

Educational 'How to' videos are some of the most discoverable on the platform. Well over 135 million 'How to' videos have been uploaded on YouTube to date![1] Creative channel *Art for Kids Hub* include *"How to draw..."* in the title of all their videos because they know viewers will be searching for popular key phrases such as *"How to draw a shark"*, that

---

1   http://youtube-trends.blogspot.com/2015/05/h-is-for-how-to-10year-sofyoutube.html

now has over 6 million views.

Another method for you to discover popular search terms is to simply type them into either Google or YouTube's search bar. Using the same format of 'How to draw a...', YouTube displays the most commonly searched phrases that can be used to influence your choice of future videos for which there is already a demand.

Recommended Videos

Recommended or Suggested videos can be another powerful source of views. These appear on the side of the watch page, below the video a viewer is currently watching on the mobile app, or as the next video to play.

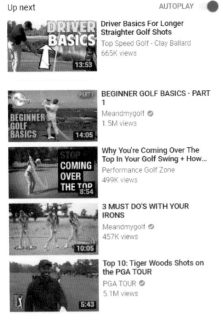

After watching a golf related video, YouTube recommended related videos from other creators

These videos are automatically generated by YouTube, targeted to entice the viewer into watching more videos. This can include videos from the same channel or from other YouTube channels.

There are a variety of factors that contribute to videos being recommended, including a viewer's past watch history, related topics, and also videos that previous viewers have watched along with the current video. To give your videos the best possible chance of being suggested by YouTube, you want to encourage your viewers to watch more of your videos. A video series can be a great way to hook viewers into binge watching multiple videos from your channel, thus increasing the likelihood of more episodes in that series being recommended to that viewer.

Home Page

Videos will appear on a viewer's home page whenever a viewer opens the YouTube app, or directly visits YouTube.com in a browser. As you can see in the example below, both videos and channels can be recommended on the Home page.

Despite countless updates over the years, the YouTube homepage is still a hub for personalised recommendations for each viewer. YouTube records over 200 million[2] different videos appearing on the Home screen every single day - that is a lot of opportunities to have your videos noticed by new viewers!

"Combat Sports" is a topic containing videos from multiple different channels based on my personal viewing habits.

"5-Minute Crafts" is a channel recommendation containing only videos from this channel.

According to YouTube's data, Subscribers tend to watch more of your videos from the home page than through the subscriptions tab.

_____

2   https://creatoracademy.youtube.com/page/lesson/discovery

However, not all videos from a viewer's subscriptions will appear on their homepage - they have to specifically visit the subscriptions tab for this.

So how can you get more of your videos to appear on the home page? YouTube surfaces videos on the home page based on two main factors:

1. Video performance - How similar viewers have engaged with the video.

2. The viewer's watch and search history - How often the viewer has watched a channel or topic area.

This means your priority should be to deliver great content for your audience, and the *more* your audience engages with your videos, the *higher* the chance your videos have of appearing on the home page of other viewers.

Trending

The trending page is a list of videos that are new and popular, specifically curated for the viewer's country. Videos are not just selected based simply on highest view count, YouTube also takes into consideration the rate of growth, where the views are coming from and other factors. There is no way to buy a placement spot on the trending page.

Access the trending tab from the drop-down left menu on YouTube.
(https://www.youtube.com/feed/trending)

As of September 2018, YouTube updated the trending tab to include five popular categories, music, live, gaming, news and movies. This allows viewers to discover trending videos within these pre-defined categories.

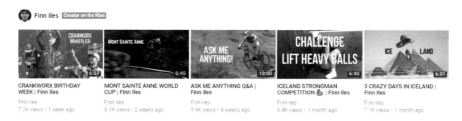

Finn Iles is a downhill mountain biker who was featured Creator on the Rise with just 7,000 subscribers!

The trending tab is also not just for popular channels. Certain countries also select a weekly 'Creator on the rise' spot in the trending tab, featuring new and upcoming creators with as little as 1,000 subscribers. Although impossible to predict, an actively growing channel that creates more broadly appealing, shareable videos is more likely to be featured in the trending tab.

Subscriptions Feed

The Subscription tab can be viewed in either a grid or list format. In the grid layout only the title and thumbnail are visible, whereas in the list format the first few lines of the description are visible

Subscribers are the viewers who enjoy your content enough to manually choose to become a subscriber of your videos. The subscriptions tab displays a list of most recent uploads from the channels a viewer has opted-in to subscribe to. Channels that are currently livestreaming will be displayed first.

Bear in mind that most viewers subscribe to many YouTube channels, so the average subscription feed is likely to have numerous videos from many other channels. Since the subscription feed is listed in chronological order (with the newest uploads appearing first) - make sure to upload your videos at times when most of your audience are most likely watching. When I lived in Australia for a period of time, I had to schedule my uploads to publish at 4:00AM Australian time to make sure I hit the peak time for the majority of my audience, who are US based!

Today

A State Of Trance Episode 881 (#ASOT881) – Armin van

Armin van Buuren ♪
6.1K watching
LIVE NOW

For Honor: Week 9/13/2018 | Weekly Content Update |

Ubisoft North America ✓
1.8K views • 1 hour ago

For Honor: Warrior's Den LIVESTREAM September 13

Ubisoft North America ✓
3.4K views •
Streamed 2 hours ago

Assassin's Creed Odyssey: Post Launch & Season Pass

Ubisoft North America ✓
23K views • 3 hours ago

Yesterday

Assassin's Creed Odyssey: Gameplay TV Spot | Ubisoft

Ubisoft North America ✓
19K views • 1 day ago

Starlink: Battle for Atlas - 4 Things You Need to Know

Ubisoft North America ✓
4.7K views • 1 day ago

The Crew® 2 Gator Rush: #LiveFromIVT– September

Ubisoft North America ✓
4.7K views •
Streamed 1 day ago

Armin VLOG #66 - Black Ops

Armin van Buuren ♪
31K views • 1 day ago

Videos from subscriptions may also appear on the home screen as well as in recommended and suggested sections by YouTube.

A trick to have your new videos appear higher in your viewer's subscription boxes, is to first upload your YouTube video as *unlisted*, and then manually change it to be *public* at 5 minutes past the hour. Since YouTube only allows videos to be scheduled *on* the hour, or 30 minutes *past* the hour - many videos will be pushed public simultaneously during each half hour slot.

For example, instead of scheduling a video to go live at 5:00PM - wait until 5:05PM to flick the video from unlisted to public. This will cause your video to go live just after all of the videos that

◉ Public

○ Members only (beta)

○ Private

○ Unlisted

DONE

were scheduled to go live at 5:00PM, resulting in your video appearing at the top of the subscription box for all your subscribers.

Notifications

By default, YouTube sends occasional notifications from channels you consistently watch or have subscribed to. This will be sent as an email notification or a push alert on mobile devices.

YouTube will *not* notify your subscribers for *every* video you upload as YouTube found this caused viewers to disable YouTube notifications completely. To be alerted for every video, a viewer must 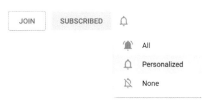 first subscribe and *then* click the notification bell next to the subscribe button.

Although notifications do not drive the majority of views for a video, they are helpful to boost the video when it initially goes public. Encourage your loyal viewers to also turn on notifications for your channel after subscribing, and that way they will not miss a video.

'Creator Insider' is an official channel, run by YouTube. I have notifications turned on for this channel so I can keep up to date with all of the latest YouTube updates.

External Sources

A viewer can discover your video outside of YouTube, as a result of: a Google Search, the video being shared on social media or even being embedded in a website, article or blog. This is called an external source.

Word of mouth is an important marketing strategy that is often overlooked. YouTube shared insights that over 50% of their core audience shares videos externally after watching them on YouTube.[3] This is an important opportunity for your video to reach new audiences and gain more views.

Give your viewers a *reason* to share your video and join the conversation. Research shows that viewers are more likely to share something if it generates an emotional response.[4] This could be happiness, surprise, admiration, satisfaction or even anger. Does your video contain a helpful 'How To' tip that viewers might want to share with their friends?

Also consider *how* people will share your video. Funny and entertaining videos can spread very effectively on platforms such as Facebook. You can also use tools such as LinkToTweet (http://www.linktotweet.com/) to make your video and a custom message easily sharable with a single click. More strategies to tap into external sources are covered in Chapter 3.

CHANNEL STRATEGY AND BOOSTING DISCOVERY

Now that we have covered where views come from, it is time to optimise your channel and content. Every YouTube channel has access to tools to increase organic discovery.

The more information you provide to YouTube about your uploads - the more data YouTube can use to determine how to surface your videos on the platform. This information is known as 'Metadata' and it is used to associate your video with related keywords. For example - if a video is about Tennis backhand swings - you want to ensure your video is shown to viewers searching for Tennis related content.

---

3   https://agency.googleblog.com/2013/05/reaching-gen-c-on-youtube.html

4   https://blog.hubspot.com/marketing/shareable-content-emotions

Video Titles

The video title is *the* most important factor in terms of search ranking on YouTube. Following this, the video description is the second most effective, and video tags are the least effective.

The first few words in your video title have more impact on SEO than the last few words in your title. So craft your video title wisely.

For example, if you are creating a gaming series, you could structure your title in sections:

> *[Video Game Title] - [Unique Keywords] (Episode Number)*

In these example titles, "*Minecraft*" is listed first to rank the video higher for this keyword than if it was listed at the end of the title. This is followed by the subject of the video to entice viewers into watching each episode. TheSyndicateProject has even capitalised "LOOKS LIKE REAL LIFE" in the title of Episode 4 to capture the attention of his viewers. The episode number is best placed at the end of the video title, as it is the least important in terms of keyword ranking.

Minecraft: The Journey Begins! - Voyage of the Deep (Hardcore) - [01]
TheSyndicateProject 1.4M views • 1 month ago
Thanks for watching! Don't forget to leave a on the video! Watch Episode 2 here . .

Minecraft: LOOKS LIKE REAL LIFE! - Voyage of the Deep (Hardcore) - [04]
TheSyndicateProject 256K views • 2 weeks ago
IT'S LIKE REAL LIFE MINECRAFT! Thanks for watching! Don't forget to leave a on the video! Make sure you're following me ...

Minecraft: The Resurrection! - Voyage of the Deep (Hardcore) - [03]
TheSyndicateProject 480K views • 4 weeks ago
'It's a new life for meeee & I'm feeeeling good!' Thanks for watching! Don't forget to leave a on the video! Make sure you're ...

TheSyndicateProject uses this formula to title each episode in his Minecraft playthrough series.

The Witcher 3 – Top 10 Tips and Tricks!
SilentcOre ⊘ 296K views • 3 years ago
The Witcher 3: Wild Hunt Gameplay! (Tips & Tricks) ☞ ☞ SUBSCRIBE HERE: http://bit.ly/TeamSilent ☜ ☜
☞ Follow me on Twitter!

"The Witcher 3" is placed at the start of this video title to have the most effect on search ranking when potential viewers searched for the name of this video game.

Posing **questions** in video titles can also be an effective way of enticing viewers to watch the video in order to discover the answer.

How much money can you possibly make at barrows?
TorvestaRS ⊘ 203K views • 1 year ago
Speed running barrows calculating how much money you can possibly make in an hour Follow me on:
Second Channel: ...

Video game creator TorvestaRS uses compelling video titles in his RuneScape videos by making his viewers wonder how much money they can make doing certain activities in the game.

EDC LAS VEGAS 2019 Ticket Unboxing
Cotton Kandi Raves • 4.4K views • 6 days ago
EDC Las Vegas 2019 Ticket Unboxing. WATCH MORE EDC VIDEOS: - EDCLV Stages:
https://youtu.be/hoZ81x9_fjA - Top 15 ...
New

Cotton Kandi Raves creates content around electronic music festivals and places an emphasis on the festival name by capitalising and placing it at the start of the video title.

A catchy title that intrigues viewers without being misleading or clickbait is key. Tricking viewers to click on your videos is never a good strategy as it will result in viewers quickly leaving and reducing your channel's Watch Time and retention rate - thus giving your videos less chance at being promoted.

BEST PRACTICES:

- Although video titles can be 100 characters long, they can get cut off at around 60-70 characters in search results, recommended videos and on mobile devices. If your video has a long title - make sure the **key details do not get clipped off.**

- Avoid using **excessive symbols** or capitalizing every word in the title - YouTube may determine that this is spam content.

- Consider the **context of your title** - YouTube can flag videos as not appropriate for all audiences if the words used are offensive, controversial or suggestive.

Video Description

In search results, the first sentence or so of your video description will be visible under the video title. Potential viewers, searching for content, will read this to better understand what a video is about and ultimately decide if they want to click on the video. Most importantly, the description box provides valuable metadata that the YouTube algorithm will use when ranking your video.

Once a viewer has clicked on your video, only the first few lines of the description are visible, so make the most of this valuable real estate. Viewers will have to click the 'show more button' to read the rest of your description, so make sure you include the most important information first.

Here are two examples from my channel that have performed well long-term. After I noticed *'How to make money'* was one of the most popular search queries for video game Grand Theft Auto Online; I decided to create a tutorial showing all the best methods.

Top 10 MONEY MAKING METHODS in GTA 5 ONLINE 2017/2018!

1,242,467 views

 Silentc0re ✓
Published on Jan 28, 2017

The best ways to make money in GTA Online/ GTA 5! If you're wondering How To Make Money in GTA Online you have come to the right place! This is my Top 10 fastest ways to make money in GTA Online today.

 Grand Theft Auto V
2013
BROWSE GAME >

SHOW MORE

The video description is crafted to include the various ways of searching 'How to make money' to help the video's discoverability when viewers are searching for this kind of content

50 HUGE Helpful Tips for Red Dead Redemption 2!

1,051,448 views

 Silentc0re ✓
Published on Nov 4, 2018

50 Useful Tips and Tricks for Red Dead Redemption 2 you should know! These Red Dead Redemption 2 Tips will substantially help your gameplay.
🔥 SUBSCRIBE HERE ▶ ▶ http://bit.ly/Silentc0re ◀ ◀

 Red Dead Redemption 2
2018
BROWSE GAME >

Although "Red Dead Redemption 2" was not entered at the start of the video title, it was reinforced twice in a natural way in the video description. Since this video was also driving a large number of new viewers I included a link to easily subscribe to my channel above the 'Show More' fold.

In this second example, I created a Tips and Tricks video around the video game 'Red Dead Redemption 2'. I anticipated a large volume of search traffic around this game at launch so I included multiple iterations of 'Red Dead Redemption 2' and 'Tips' to provide YouTube with the metadata it needed to surface this video for an audience searching for Tips for Red Dead Redemption 2.

BEST PRACTICES:

- Take time to **customise** your video description for each video you upload. Start off the description with 1-2 sentences describing what the video is about.

- Do not be afraid to **repeat** what the video title is in the description to reinforce the keywords to make your video more searchable. Create search friendly sentences by using keywords in natural language to avoid being flagged for spam.

- Decide what information you want **to prioritise at the top of the description box,** and what information is better suited for below the fold (under the '*show more*' button). It is important the text visible at the top includes the information you want your viewers to see first. Such as including a link to Subscribe to your channel, or a link to another video, or if you have a website or product that you want to drive traffic to.

- The description box allows for up to **5,000 characters** in total - this leaves room to add links to other videos you think viewers would enjoy from your channel, your social media pages, a website or a brief bio about yourself and channel.

- Add a **related Hashtag** (#) to your video description to help the video rank when users search for specific hashtags. However do not add too many hashtags to your video description or else YouTube will ignore all of them!

- Do not list **irrelevant words** in the description, or write a list of 'tags' in the video description - this is against YouTube's Community Guidelines and Terms of Service and risks your video being removed.

Do not forget you can create **default descriptions** (see below) to save you having to re-enter the same information into each video you upload. For example, if you like to link all your social media pages in the description - you can make this your default description and then enter the unique information for each video above the default text.

How to set default descriptions:

1. Sign into YouTube and visit your creator studio (https://studio.youtube.com)

2. Select Settings from the left menu

3. Edit upload defaults

Video Tags

Although not as effective for ranking in search as the video title and description; entering relevant tags and keywords into the tags section will help your videos get discovered.

Consider what keywords or phrases your target audience is searching for and separate each word or phrase with a comma. It can also help to enter tags that replicate the various ways viewers may be searching about a certain topic. Personally, I like to reinforce tags with popular search terms that are relevant to the video.

This video was a vlog introducing my new Border Collie puppy. I used common phrases related to dogs and puppies in the tags field starting with the most relevant. Currently, this video still ranks within the few videos when you search '*Border Collie Puppy*' on YouTube.

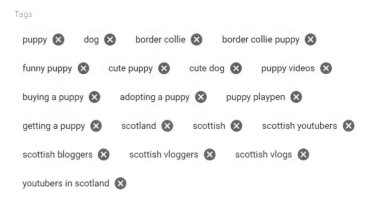

Prioritise your tags - The first few words or phrases in the tags section are the most important in terms of ranking

- List the most **important and relevant tags first**.
- Use a **combination** of single words and phrases.
- YouTube allows up to **500 characters** in the tags section - use them all!
- It is common for viewers to search for content with incorrect spelling - try adding in commonly **misspelled tags**.

- Experiment using both **British and American English** words and phrases. There are also spelling differences such as 'Colour' in British English, which is spelled 'Color' in American English.

- Similar to titles and descriptions, **misleading tags are a policy violation** and should be avoided. Using misleading tags will also affect your video ranking as those viewers will not engage with your video, reducing the chances of YouTube surfacing it for other users.

Thumbnails

Thumbnails are usually the *first* thing people see. YouTube report that 90% of the best performing videos on the platform use custom thumbnails.[5] Rather than YouTube automatically generating a thumbnail, taking the time to create a custom thumbnail can be the difference between a viewer clicking on your video, or simply scrolling past it.

Thumbnails are also part of your overall channel branding. Finding a unique style or format will allow viewers to identify what videos are yours from the thumbnail alone. Sometimes I actually spend more time creating a thumbnail than the actual video took me to make!

Instead of operating independently, think about your title, description and thumbnail all working together to tell a story and better illustrate your content to viewers. In search results, viewers will be able to see all three.

The most important factor is to ensure your thumbnail accurately represents your video contents. If you have tricked someone into clicking on a thumbnail expecting something - such as a trailer for

---

5   https://creatoracademy.youtube.com/page/lesson/thumbnails

Grand Theft Auto 9 (that does not yet exist), viewers will leave almost immediately. YouTube rewards videos with discoverability that encourage viewers to keep watching, so it is in your best interests to ensure viewers who click on your video, stay to watch it through.

Here are 5 solid strategies that YouTube's top channels use to create more clickable thumbnails:

Playstation Access uses a **consistent** blue template for their thumbnails, allowing viewers to easily identify their videos.

Jelly effectively uses very **bright and fun** thumbnails, that stand out and draws the attention of his viewers.

Ali-A is primarily a gaming channel, however he appears in most of his thumbnails displaying **strong facial emotions**. Viewers are more likely to click on a video if they become connected to an emotion.

The Sidemen channel regularly uses **outlines** to make the subjects stand out from the background.

The Game Theorists use **close ups** of both real life faces and video game characters. Humans are instinctively drawn to eye contact and close ups can make thumbnails extremely eye catching, even when displayed small on mobile devices

BEST PRACTICES:

- **High quality**: Edit your thumbnails in a high resolution (at least 1280x720 pixels) and the correct aspect ratio for YouTube (16:9).

- **File Size**: YouTube has a thumbnail size limit of 2MB. If you are unable to use .PNG due to the file size, .JPG allows a greater range of compression.

- **Keep text concise**: Too much text on thumbnails can be off-putting for some viewers - especially if the text only repeats what is in the title of the video. Make sure your text is also eligible when thumbnails are shrunk down to the smallest size - such as on mobile devices.

- **Close ups**: Close up shots of faces tend to work best - this can be real life faces, animals or even video game characters!

- **Sometimes less is more**: although your thumbnail might look great when editing full screen in Photoshop - once it's shrunk down, does it still look as visually appealing?

- **Size matters**: Preview your video thumbnail and title combination on a mobile device to make sure it works as effectively as it does on a PC or laptop.

- **Use images safe for all audiences**: Avoid shocking, offensive, violent, indecent or misleading characteristics as this can cause your video to be ranked lower and less likely for YouTube to recommend it to new viewers.

Playlists

If you are not already organising your videos into playlists you are missing out! Playlists allow you to organise groups of videos on your channel to maintain the correct ordering, as well as allowing you to share a group of your videos, rather than just one.

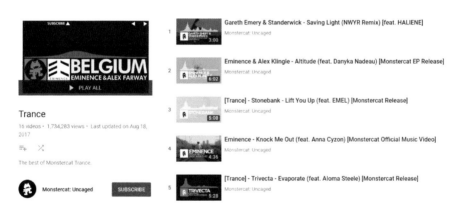

Music label *Monstercat* use playlists to group videos of
each music genre into playlists - this helps retain viewers
within Monstercat's uploads

The most powerful aspect of Playlists is they automatically play in a pre-arranged order until the viewer stops. This means after a viewer has finished watching one of your videos, instead of selecting another video to watch that may come from another YouTube channel - the playlist will automatically select the next video in the playlist. This can greatly increase the number of videos your viewers watch in a row, thus increasing your channel's overall Watch Time ranking.

BEST PRACTICES:

- Keep your playlists **organised** by relevant content categories to ensure the next video to play will be related to the previously watched videos.

- Instead of sharing a single video on social media or with friends - **share the playlist link** to increase repeat viewership.

- Create a **'Best of' Playlist'** and feature it on your channel's homepage so new viewers will see your best work.

- Playlists can also appear in search results and suggested videos - so make sure you **include relevant keywords** in the Playlist's title and description.

Cards

Cards are interactive links that can be added to a video once it has been uploaded on YouTube. You can add up to 5 cards per video and they will appear on both browser and mobile. They are not as intrusive to the viewer experience as their predecessor (Video Annotations) - so feel free to add at least one to every video you upload!

You can use cards to direct viewers to other videos, playlists, channels and even run polls. If you are a YouTube Partner (more about that soon)

- you can also link to approved websites or even your own website after it has been approved as an 'Associated Website' on your Google Account. YouTube also has an extensive list of approved third party merchandise and crowdfunding websites that can be linked directly from your cards.

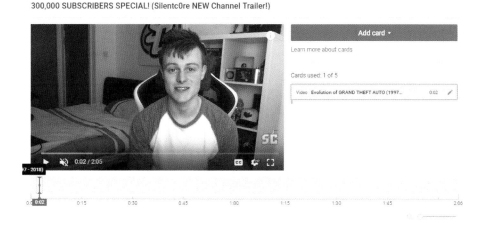

Cards will appear in the top right corner of your video - viewers can click the (i) to expand the contents

How to enable Cards:

1. Visit your Video Manager (https://www.youtube.com/my_videos)

2. Edit the video you want to add a card to

3. Click the Cards tab

4. Select the type of card you want to add

Make sure your cards appear at the most relevant time within the video. If you are using a card to direct your viewers to another video, try not to set them to appear in the most exciting part of the video as they may not want to leave! Cards are most effective towards the end portion of a video when viewers are getting ready to leave.

- Always give a **verbal call-to-action** with each card - this will substantially increase viewer engagement.
- Regularly use **poll cards** on your videos - it is a great way to increase viewer engagement on your content. I used this feature to ask my viewers if they play Xbox or Playstation, the 'best console' debate continued into the comment section which was great for engagement!

TRANSLATIONS

You want to make it as easy as possible for international viewers to find your channel and consume more of your content by improving their viewer experience.

The potential for a worldwide audience is largely dependent on the kind of content you make and how appealing it is to audiences in different countries. Cooking and DIY content for example have huge potential to a worldwide audience, as almost everyone can relate to cooking and crafting at home.

YouTube is now localised in over 100 countries and can be accessed in 80 different languages.[6].There are several tools available to help your videos reach international audiences such as captions, subtitles, and translated titles and descriptions. These tools are also useful for any viewers who have difficulty hearing, who are watching in a public,

---

6   https://www.youtube.com/yt/about/press/

who are watching in a noisy environment, or even if they are watching without sound.

Closed Captions and Subtitles:

This is a written transcript of a video that viewers can choose to display on-screen. Some viewers prefer to read words instead of listen to them and closed captions are a quick and easy option to add to your channel. YouTube can also auto-generate captions in some languages, although if you have a Scottish accent like me it is sometimes easier said than done!

How to enable Closed Captions/Subtitles:

1. Visit your Video Manager (https://www.youtube.com/my_videos)
2. Edit the video you want to add captions or subtitles to
3. Click the Subtitles/CC Tab
4. Select the language you want to add

For my channel I selected English, and then checked the box to make that the default option for all new uploads.

Translated Metadata:

This increases discoverability of your videos to viewers that speak languages other than your own. You should use this in conjunction with subtitles of the same language. For example, this would allow a French viewer to not only find your video, but also watch it with French subtitles!

There are two ways to translate your video titles and descriptions, either translate them yourself, or enable **Community Contributions** - a feature that allows your community to help!

Community Contributions:

Having to manually do translations on every video would be a huge task - but thankfully YouTube allows for community contributions! This allows the YouTube community to help contribute closed captions, subtitles and translated metadata; such as titles and descriptions for your videos. The submissions will then go through a review process, where you can either review and approve the contributions, or you can leave it to other viewers to confirm their accuracy, and YouTube will automatically publish them live. If you notice any inaccuracies in published translations - you can always go back and edit them later.

As your audience grows on YouTube, you are likely to gain viewers who speak other languages. An estimated 80% of YouTube views come from outside of the United States.[7] Community contributions are a great way for your followers to provide a better multilingual experience on your videos and help you reach a more worldwide audience.

You may be wondering, *well how can I get people to contribute*? The first step is to just ask! You may already have multilingual viewers watching, that you did not know about who would be happy to help. Channels that have a close relationship with their viewers can benefit from their dedicated fans who want to help make the videos more accessible in their own language. Contributors can also opt in to be credited in the video description with a link to their own channel!

You can further incentivise contributions by giving verbal shout-outs within your videos or awarding prizes to top contributors. Simply making yourself available is also a great way to connect directly with your contributors. So start up a group chat with your contributors - thank them for their hard work, answer any questions they may

---

7   https://www.forbes.com/sites/hughmcintyre/2017/04/14/despite-gains-with-streaming-youtube-is-still-how-the-world-listens-to-music

have, and cultivate a team of active translators who may be willing to translate your upcoming videos.

How to enable Community Contributions:

1. Sign into YouTube and visit your creator studio (https://studio.youtube.com)

2. Select Transcriptions from the left menu

3. Click the community tab and 'Turn on for all videos'

If you want to opt out specific videos from community contributions, you can disable individual videos within the Video Manager settings.

CHAPTER 2 CHECKLIST

If you are wondering why your channel is not growing or netting views, here are the best ways of optimising your channel:

- ☐ *Optimise Video: Titles, Description and Tags for Search*

- ☐ *Use custom thumbnails to intrigue viewers and make them click*

- ☐ *Create category Playlists*

- ☐ *Include End Screens and Cards*

- ☐ *Provide Translations and Community Contributions*

CHAPTER 3

BUILDING VIEWERSHIP MOMENTUM

There are now over 1.9 billion users who visit YouTube every month, and that just the users who have logged in![8]

Building a community on YouTube relies on your momentum on the platform. Channels can disappear quicker than they were established so it is essential to stay in tune with your audience.

*Growing a successful channel comes in two parts; bringing in **new viewers** while also **maintaining current viewers.** You may think by uploading videos these two objectives will always be simultaneously satisfied. However, in practice you need to find a balance. For instance, creating content that is extremely searchable and brings in new viewers - might not necessarily be what your core audience wants to watch. On the other hand, question and answers (QnA videos) may be highly engaging for your core audience, but unlikely to bring in a plethora of new subscribers.*

---

8   https://youtube-creators.googleblog.com/2018/07/mid-year-update-on-our-five-creator.html

INCLUDED IN CHAPTER 3

- ☑ *Kick-start your channel on YouTube*
- ☑ *Why subscribers are important*
- ☑ *Convert your views to susbcribers*
- ☑ *Programming*
- ☑ *Collaborating*
- ☑ *Local networking*
- ☑ *Social Media Amplification*
- ☑ *Foster a positive community*
- ☑ *Persistence and Sustainability*

KICK-START YOUR CHANNEL ON YOUTUBE

If you have not already started uploading content on your YouTube channel, the first step is to just start! Most people postpone starting out as they tend to overthink if they have the right microphone, the best camera setup or good enough editing skills. The truth is, your first few videos will probably suck. But that is ok. With each video you create, you are advancing your production skills and building your own confidence on the platform. Each video you make will become easier, you will be more efficient at editing and more in tune with what formats work. If you do get embarrassed with your early amateur videos, you can always go back and delete them later - or what I like to do is make them private so I can go back and have a good laugh about how awkward I was!

Making your first video will be daunting. However, by posting it you will already be ahead of 92% of people who set goals they never fulfil.[9] Most people who say they want be a YouTuber - never actually make any progress beyond the thought of it.

How to create an impactful First Video:

- **Introduce yourself** - Keep it simple, create an introduction video explaining who you are.

- **Channel goals** - Explain what you want to be known for - what your channel aims to accomplish.

- **Who is your audience** - What kind of people do you envision watching your videos.

- **Who inspires you** - What or who inspired you to create your channel in the first place.

---

9   https://www.inc.com/marcel-schwantes/science-says-92-percent-of-peo-ple-dont-achieve-goals-heres-how-the-other-8-perce.html

WHY SUBSCRIBERS ARE IMPORTANT

Subscribers are critical to any channel's success on YouTube. Although you can focus entirely on increasing view counts, subscribers actually spend more time watching your videos than casual non-subscribers. So nurturing your subscriber base is essential, as they will be the ones to help build momentum on your channel.

Your subscribers are your core audience and will provide important initial signals to YouTube that will impact how it performs on the platform. Growing a subscriber base that engages with your new videos will help improve the lifespan of your video and make it more discoverable to a new audience.

100 Subscribers

There is no denying that your first 100 Subscribers to your channel will be a hustle. Tell all your friends who have a YouTube channel to Subscribe. Be vocal at family events and let them know you are pursuing a YouTube channel and how important their support can be to aiding your growth at the beginning.

Although Subscriber growth is important, this part of your journey should also be spent curating the best content possible. This is also a great time to experiment with your channel. Once you have an established audience, trying new things can be more problematic because your viewers have certain expectations. So take advantage of being able to try different formats and editing styles, and aim to improve your production quality with each video.

1,000 Subscribers

Once you have reached your first 100 Subscribers, naturally your next goal should be the big 1,000. By now your channel should have a concise purpose and direction, and your video content should have a clear schedule.

Once you reach the 1,000 milestone, new viewers to your channel are more likely to take you more seriously as they can see you are an upcoming YouTuber with a growing audience. This will help with furthering your channel's growth and even collaborating with similar creators.

10,000 Subscribers

Your commitment to the grind will be a big deciding factor of how quickly you can grow your audience to this level. I would recommend breaking this up into mini-goals of each 1,000 subscribers until you reach the 10K mark.

Accumulating 10,000 subscribers will likely be a long journey in your YouTuber career. However, the good news is that with each 1,000 subscribers you gain, your channel should be gaining momentum and hitting milestones faster.

100,000 subscribers

This is a huge milestone to hit, as YouTube will officially recognise your achievement with a personal letter and physical silver play button you can hang on your wall! Better still, YouTube rewards you with a gold and diamond play buttons for hitting 1 million subscribers and 10 million subscribers respectively.

CONVERT YOUR VIEWS TO SUBSCRIBERS

The bulk of YouTube creator's views actually come from non-subscribers. Since subscribers have been shown to consume twice as much video as non-subscribers, your goal should be to convert as many of these passive viewers into fans as possible.

Here are my Top 10 methods to convert views to subscribers.

1. Ask them to subscribe!

Have you ever gone on a long binge of watching random YouTube videos? When viewers are passively consuming content, it is easy for them to transition into another video that may be from another channel (YouTube's auto-play feature will also automatically switch to the next related video if enabled). Simply asking viewers to Subscribe to your channel is a great way to remind them before they leave.

This does not mean spending 2 minutes at the start of every video begging viewers to like and subscribe before the content has even started (this has unfortunately become common in some communities). Not only will you turn away potential viewers, but hinder subscribers you have already gained as they will want to get into the content.

Strategically place your call-to-actions within your content, such as just after the video's focal point or a funny moment to capture the viewer's highest sentiment. For a more gentle approach - simply ask your viewers to subscribe in a genuine way, explaining both the benefits to them in doing so and even how it supports you as a creator can go a long way.

I like to include a call-to-action in the outro of all my videos - if a viewer has watched one of my videos all the way through, there is a good chance they will want more.

2. Create a repeatable series to be remembered

One-off videos can perform great independently, however once the video is finished viewers tend to move on. Your long-term success lies within the format of a repeatable show. It can also help having a consistent personality throughout the series to build a sense of familiarity and expectation from your fans.

When starting out as a small creator, it is often easier to become known for a specific series, than known as a channel. For example, when I was creating videos for video game *Grand Theft Auto*, it was not my one-off videos that drove most of my growth in subscribers, it was my repeatable weekly series. I was able to continue a weekly series for several years creating well over 100 episodes. Have you had any one-off videos perform exceptionally well on your channel that you could develop into a repeatable show?

Daily Observations   PLAY ALL
Things that happen during my daily riding in London

Daily Observations 245	Daily Observations 244	Daily Observations 243	Daily Observations 242	Daily Observations 241
RoyalJordanian ✓	RoyalJordanian ✓	RoyalJordanian ✓	RoyalJordanian ✓	RoyalJordanian ✓
133K views · 1 week ago	105K views · 3 weeks ago	181K views · 1 month ago	98K views · 2 months ago	146K views · 2 months ago

If you are a bit of a procrastinator like myself, having a regular series can actually force you into being more productive!

Royal Jordanian is a motorcycle fanatic with all his content revolving around bikes. He uses a helmet-mounted action camera to capture random encounters from sighting rare cars to funny pedestrian reactions to him almost being bike-jacked by a gang of thieves. These moments are compiled into a regular show on his channel called '*Daily Observations*' that now has over 200 episodes. Despite not even searching for motorbikes when I accidently stumbled across one of these videos - I ended up binge watching a bunch of episodes and then decided to subscribe! These episodes routinely perform better than his one-off content episodes by hooking viewers into watching more.

One of my favourite channels to watch at the moment is *Girlfriend Reviews*. Each video is a well-crafted review of video games and films, from a girlfriend's perspective. Although each video is about a completely different video game or film, the girlfriend review is the repeatable format. Her viewers know exactly what to expect, and are likely to come back for more if they enjoy the format. By following a schedule of just one upload per week, her channel grew by over 400,000 subscribers in just 4 months!

Finding a unique content format that can be easily duplicated will grow your active viewer base and keep them hooked.

3. Set goals with your viewers

Let your viewers feel like they are a part of your experience. Set goals and celebrate with your viewers when you reach them. Creating special videos for reaching goals such as your first 100 subscribers is a great way to give back and thank your audience for helping you achieve it.

Make your viewers feel special if they were among your first 100 or 1,000 subscribers. This will encourage fans into supporting you longer and seeing you reach more goals.

ExplodingTNT creates Minecraft videos and set a viewer goal of 5,000,000 subscribers for him to release a voice reveal! Keeping his identify hidden, gives his channel an element of mystery and keeps viewers wanting to know more. Viewers love to get to know the people behind the channels they watch - can you build anticipation for a face reveal on your channel?

4. Be authentic and relatable

The audience on YouTube is different than other forms of media. If something is forced, or unnatural, viewers will definitely sense that.

Viewers are looking to have a unique connection with the creators they follow. Sharing personal stories, struggles or experiences will make you more relatable to many people. *Boogie2988* is a gaming personality on YouTube who regularly shares his weight loss journey. Leaving viewers with an inspirational message will make them want to come back.

Being relatable can also come in the form of your environment or video backdrop. I always record my YouTube videos in my bedroom which is much more relatable to my audience than if I rented an office space. Whenever I upgrade a certain aspect of my setup such as a new microphone - I like to show my audience and get them excited for an increased video quality. Stay true to your audience!

5. Be memorable with Channel Traditions

Having consistent traditions unique to your channel will keep your viewers coming back for more. Develop a catchphrase you use regularly, a code name you call your fans or even the way you introduce your videos. This will make your viewers feel like they are a part of a special insider community.

One of my favourite traditions is from gaming creator *Slayermusiq1*, who abruptly ends every video with "*k-thanks-bye*". If an occasional video does not include the traditional outro - his viewers will actually be upset!

Your traditions can also be content related, such as having a comment of the week where you give a mention to your favourite comment from a previous video. Try hosting a regular podcast, livestream or 'Fun Friday' hang out, where you spend an hour answering questions or playing games with your fans.

6. Grow a community

Focus on the community building aspect of your channel. You are bringing together a group of people who share similar beliefs and passions. No matter what content subject your channel is based around - lifestyle vlogs to video games, there will be communities out there to tap into. Having a deeper connection with your audience and giving them positive interactions on your channel is key to long-term growth.

Building a community does not happen overnight, so stay positive and maintain a community that people will want to get involved in. Word of mouth is a powerful discoverability tool - giving one viewer a positive experience could result in them sharing your video with a friend who shares the same passion points.

When I first upload a video I try to respond to some of the first comments. This encourages viewers to leave more comments if they see a creator is interacting - further boosting the video's engagement!

As a creator, you can really make someone's day by responding to their comments!

7. Recognise your biggest fans

You may start to recognise the same names interacting with your videos, be sure to acknowledge them! If someone is taking the time to engage with several of your videos - make them feel special. These are the loyal fans that will talk about you and help share your videos.

This is an advantage that small creators can have over large creators who receive a high volume of comments. Be memorable by giving them a unique experience they can only get on *your* channel. One of my fans was so happy that I liked his comment he actually uploaded a video the same day titled *"SILENTCORE LIKED MY COMMENT"*, where he said how happy it made him that one of his favourite YouTubers noticed him. Take a few minutes to respond to fan feedback on each video you upload, a simple action or gesture can go a long way.

8. Involve your audience in your creation process

Encourage your viewers to leave you feedback to help you improve your content. This could be on all aspects of the content such as feedback on your new video series, the quality of the lighting or sound, or even the background music you use.

You may also find dedicated fans leaving great ideas or concepts for future content. I have quite often sourced awesome video ideas from the comments section on my videos. Be sure to acknowledge anyone if you use their suggestion. Imagine how you would feel if your favourite Netflix TV show decided to incorporate one of your ideas into a future episode and personally thank you for it!

This viewer made a suggestion for a future video, he was happy to see that I not only used his idea, but also thanked him personally within the video!

Highlighted comment

Oliver Mason 7 months ago

Hey, you did my idea! :)

👍 2 👎 💬 REPLY

Involving your audience in your channel and videos is a great way to get them invested in your content. Rather than passively watching your content, they will feel empowered that their voices are being heard. *'Honest Trailers'* is a weekly series by *Screen Junkies* where a deep-voiced narrator parodies popular movie trailers. They involve their audience by taking suggestions for future film suggestions to parody, and feature those users who suggested the film within the episode. In the outro of these videos the narrator then reads fun comments from the previous episode, further integrating their fans within the content and subsequently increasing the engagement in the comment section of their videos. Is there a way you could integrate a featured comment within your content?

9. Spark a Conversation with your fans

Making your videos conversational will help build a stronger bond between you and your fans. At the recording stage, try not to just talk *at* your audience, but intentionally drive a conversation *with* your audience. Consider the difference between the way a news reporter will talk on the television, to the way your favourite YouTube creator will communicate within their videos. This might feel weird at first, but it can help if you imagine you are talking to a close friend when recording your videos.

The conversation also does not end when the video is uploaded. The first few hours when a video goes live are the most impactful to interact with fans in the comments section. When viewers see that a creator has been engaging with other viewers, they are more likely to leave a comment themselves and join the conversation.

As a small creator, make it your priority to reply to every single comment you receive on YouTube. Replying to comments is a proven way to invest in your community. Make them feel important and value their input and they are more likely to stick around. As your community grows you may no longer have time to respond to every comment, but you can still give comments a thumbs up by hitting the like icon or a heart to show your appreciation. They will be notified. Even if I receive over 100 comments on a video I will still take the time to heart as many as I can to let my audience know that I have read their message. Although this can be time consuming I often receive messages from delighted fans that I have taken the time to heart their comment.

You can also pin a comment to the top of the comments section. This will be the first comment your fans will see when viewing your video, so choose carefully! Pinning comments can be a great way to guide a conversation or ask a question of your audience.

> You can only pin one comment per video,
> but it will appear above all other comments.

Bookmark the Community Comments Tab so you can regularly review new comments across all your videos in one place (https://www.youtube.com/comments). Do not forget to check the Spam filter as sometimes legitimate comments will get caught up in the 'Spam' and 'Held for Review' tabs. The official YouTube Creator Studio app is another great way to keep up with comments on the go.

10. Always be there

If you are taking extended breaks from YouTube and social media, viewers can quickly forget about you. I managed to experience this first hand when I decided to take a 3 month break from uploading videos - and my active viewership was more than halved on my return. Ouch!

Posting content consistently is the first step towards always being there for your audience. However it does not end there, maintaining an active online presence between uploads will keep you fresh in the minds of your viewers. Reply to new questions or comments left on your videos to keep your audience engaged. If you have access to YouTube's Community tab (Accessed by clicking 'Community' on your channel's homepage), this is another way to interact with your followers by sharing status updates, images, GIFs, polls or even your favourite YouTube videos. I often re-share my new uploads the day after I uploaded them to reach viewers who may have missed it the first time in their news feed.

Utilise social media to let your fans know what you are working on, share behind-the-scenes photos or a sneak peek at what video will be released next. This will help drive traffic back to your channel on a regular basis.

Comment Filters

You can add a list of blocked words and phrases that will automatically filter-out any new matching comments on your channel. Any words or phrases from your blocked words list will not show up publicly on your channel and will be held for a manual review. If you want to keep your channel family friendly, you could have a fun brainstorming session to find every offensive word or phrase you can think of to add into this section and have your filters maintain a clean comment section.

Filters can be used to avoid any particularly sensitive topics being discussed in your community. I occasionally receive comments stating that I need to get a better haircut (they are probably right) - so if I wanted to prevent this I could add *"haircut"* as a blocked word and any comments containing this word would be automatically filtered.

How to blacklist specific words:

1. Sign into YouTube and visit your creator studio (https://studio. youtube.com)

2. Select Settings from the left menu

3. Click Community and scroll down to Blocked words

Community Moderators

If any friends or regular fans that you trust are willing to help manage your channel, you can assign comment moderators. Moderators will have the ability to hide comments on your channel for your final review. This will be particularly important if you livestream to allow you to concentrate on the video content and have moderators stay on top of the chat.

How to assign Moderators:

1. Sign into YouTube and visit your creator studio (https://studio.youtube.com)

2. Select Settings from the left menu

3. Click Community and add moderators by channel URL

How to handle Negativity

When it comes to dealing with negative comments online, it is in your best interests to sensitively handle the situation. This goes for any business venture or career. When you start to find success there will always be individuals who will not agree or simply derive pleasure in attempting to bring other people down.

It is also worth bearing in mind that the kind of people that spend their day spewing negative or hateful comments online, are likely not in a happy and positive environment themselves. They could be a victim of bullying and perhaps use online trolling as an escape from their own issues. A knee-jerk reaction might be to tell them to take a hike. However, sometimes a more sensitive approach can defuse a situation. Understand that this is something that *all* YouTube creators encounter. It is how you choose to respond that reflects on *you* as a creator.

I have also found that many 'haters' are not actually expecting a reply from a creator. When I have replied to negative comments they are sometimes followed up with a response such as *"Omg he replied!"*

or *"Respect for replying, subbed"*. By offering a little attention you can change the tone of the conversation into a more constructive or positive interaction, and can even result in them becoming a future fan!

If a comment does violate any of YouTube's Community Guidelines, you can always flag the message to YouTube.

PROGRAMMING

Most creators will tell you one of the most important principles of running a successful YouTube channel is consistency. What they mean by this is setting a regular programming strategy and an upload schedule that your viewers can expect from you. Think of your YouTube channel like your favourite TV show. If you tune in each week for the latest TV episode - how would you feel if all of a sudden it did not show with no explanation?

Video Programming

Having a regular upload schedule does not mean uploading daily for two weeks straight, and then taking a three month break. Create an upload schedule that is both achievable, and also realistic from the time commitments you allocate to creating content. Setting an overly ambitious schedule can cause you to become burned out. If you are not happy creating your content - your audience will sense this. Take into consideration any outside commitments you may have, such as a full-time job, family or school. Decide how many hours you are able to dedicate to your YouTube channel on a regular basis.

Your upload schedule is also likely to vary, based on the type of content you are creating. Gaming playthrough channels for example, tend to have a more frequent upload schedule as they are able to record multiple videos in one sitting. On the other hand, channels that require a high level of production or post-production may have to set a more staggered schedule.

FK Films creates Stop Motion Animations using LEGO. The channel has a strict upload schedule of every second Friday. The channel banner is regularly updated with the date of the next episode.

Be sure to regularly promote your schedule to your audience and let them know when to return to your channel for the next video. As your active viewer base grows you can also gauge if there is an appetite for more content.

Channel Programming

You might have noticed some large YouTube creators on the platform running multiple YouTube channels simultaneously to hit different niches. *Maxmoefoe* runs four different YouTube channels, three of which have over 1,000,000 subscribers! There are also beauty and lifestyle creators that have secondary channels to share gaming videos.

maxmoefoe	maxmoefoetwo	maxmoefoegames	maxmoefoePokemon
2,940,291 subscribers	1,623,991 subscribers	1,657,033 subscribers	983,788 subscribers
SUBSCRIBE	SUBSCRIBE	SUBSCRIBE	SUBSCRIBE

This is not as easy as it looks, as managing just one YouTube channel properly is a huge challenge. Unless you have a dedicated editor and a production team, running multiple successful channels will be astronomically more difficult.

It is a common misconception to think that starting out with multiple YouTube channels, producing different kinds of content, will grow faster than one. Opening numerous YouTube channels may mean spreading yourself too thinly - most likely resulting in you running several channels poorly than one channel at its full potential.

I was once contacted by a creator who requested advice on why his YouTube channel was not growing. After reviewing his content I noticed he had four different YouTube channels he was trying to run simultaneously, despite none of them even reaching 100 Subscribers! Instead of running all four channels poorly, I advised that he selected one and streamlined his efforts.

This is not to say that you should *never* launch a secondary YouTube channel, but you should first focus your efforts on establishing one main channel. Once you build an engaged audience, who love and support your content on one channel, it will be much easier to cross-pollinate between channels.

BEST PRACTICES:

- Maintain **a healthy schedule** that will continue to ignite your passion in the subject.

- Communicate your **programming schedule** regularly. Mention it in videos and advertise it on your channel's banner for any newcomers to your channel.

- If you are uploading on a weekly basis, **select a set day to upload** to structure your uploads.

- If you are going on holiday you can **prepare videos ahead of time** and schedule them in the creator studio to upload in advance. Otherwise, if you do need to break your schedule - let your fans know!

- Only create secondary YouTube channels if you have the **time and resources** to maintain them alongside your main channel.

COLLABORATING

Collaborating with other YouTube channels is a fantastic way to reach new viewers as well as strengthen your strategic relationships and partnerships on the platform with other creators. This can come in a few forms from simple shoutouts to another YouTube channel, to full on collaborative appearances within videos.

YouTube collaborations seem to have a bit of a stigma that you can only work with other creators that have a similar subscriber count. While having more subscribers can make you more attractive to potential collaborators, it is often not a deal breaker.

Before reaching out to any other YouTubers, it is important to first have your channel established. I have heard a few creators say *"After we collaborate and I get some subscribers, then I'll make videos"*. This does not work for a few reasons. Firstly, you bring no value to the table for other creators to collaborate with; that is like applying to a job and telling them you will send them your resume after they hire you! Secondly, even if you do manage to find someone to collaborate with, viewers are unlikely to subscribe when they visit your channel and see it is inactive.

So before doing any reach outs, make sure your channel looks visually appealing. Work through the checklist outlined in Chapter 2 to best optimise your channel and ensure you have a clear channel mission statement and goal. This will not only help any potential collaborators understand what your channel is all about, but give any new viewers that visit your channel as a result of the collaboration, the best possible experience and a reason to subscribe. Uploading regular content on your channel will also show that you are an active channel, and even having a small viewer base will help other creators understand if your audiences could be a good alignment.

Start small

Remember the larger the channel you are reaching out to, the more inundated they will be with collaboration requests.

Do not be opposed to working with channels smaller than you. Although they may be smaller in reach, they could have extremely dedicated fans that will cross-over and support your channel. Dedicated smaller channels can also grow in size rapidly, so establishing a good relationship with them early will be invaluable. If you help a smaller creator get a foothold on YouTube - they will most certainly want to return the favour in the future.

Reaching Out

When reaching out to creators to line up any potential collaborations, your pitch is crucial. Make sure you actually spend time assessing their channel, get familiar with the types of content they make and who the personality (or personalities) are behind the channel.

Here is an example of a great sample pitch I received:

> *"Hey Dan,*
>
> *I really enjoyed your Watch Dogs gaming series. I also run a channel that covers the Watch Dogs series (1k subs) and would love to work with you on a video.*
>
> *I have a new idea for a video using the game that could work on both our channels. We could be one of the first ones to cover this in a video*
>
> *If you are interested you can message me on Twitter, I already follow you"*

This is a great pitch for a few reasons. He addresses my real name rather than my YouTube Alias - clearly he has spent time reading my bio. He references specific videos I have worked on, so he must have spent time watching my content. Since we both create similar videos about the same video game, there could definitely be some synergy there with our audiences. Most importantly, he also proposes a unique idea that could benefit us both, so I am already interested in hearing more. He finishes his proposal with the best platform to contact him on, making connecting with him as easy as possible.

In comparison - Here are a few examples of some not-so-great pitches I have received:

> *"Hey man. I was wondering if you could give me a shoutout on your channel?"*

This sounds like a very one-sided collaboration proposal... Unfortunately, I had to decline.

> *"Wanna collab?"*

This was his whole email, seriously.

Cross Promotion

At the end of the day, the goal for your collaboration is to cross-promote between your audiences. This can be done with a simple shoutout to another channel within your video, or even better - upload two different videos to each of your individual channels. That way your audiences have a reason to migrate from one channel to the other.

Within your collaboration video, be sure to ask any new viewers to subscribe to your channel! This is a great way to maintain some new viewers as a result of the collaboration and convert them into new subscribers.

Lastly, it is good manners to link the channel you are collaborating with towards the top of your video description (as opposed to below the fold - see Description in Chapter 1). You can also use cards and an end screen to link directly to the collaborators channel and make it as easy as possible for any potential viewers to cross pollinate between your channels.

BEST PRACTICES:

- **Do your personalities fit**? Make sure your collaborators are compatible with your channel. If the collaboration feels forced or awkward, your audiences will sense that.

- **Do not copy and paste** the same collaboration proposal to everyone. Make it personal, familiarise yourself with their channel and videos. Compliment the creator on what aspects of their channel you like - and why you want to collaborate with them.

- **Include a value proposition** - Do you have access to a studio, production equipment, exclusive locations or a unique viewer base that may be attractive to a potential collaborator?

- **Include an idea in your pitch** - How do you plan on collaborating? For a busy creator, having a great collaboration proposal can be the difference between replying or scrolling past to the next email.

- **Cross-promote** - after the collaboration, make the most of cross promoting your audiences. Actively encourage your viewers to check out the creator you are collaborating with. Link their channel, tag them in your social media posts and they are likely to do the same in return. Ending your collaboration on a positive note, will leave you open to future collaborations with that creator, as well as being a good example of how you can work with any other channels.

LOCAL NETWORKING

Depending where you are geographically located in the world, you may have an active community of creators in your local area! This is a great way to exchange knowledge, make connections for collaborations, or simply just make some new friends!

While living in Australia I discovered a very active Facebook community called "*Australian YouTubers*" with over 5,000 members. The group contains a helpful community, welcoming related questions from new creators and also hosting regular meet-ups.

My home country, Scotland, also has an active creator community with local group "*Create Scotland*" that now has over 1,000 Discord (https://www.discordapp.com) members.

Meetup (https://www.meetup.com/) is an online service used to create and organize online communities. It is worthwhile searching for any existing groups in your local city. If you cannot find one in your area - consider creating one!

SOCIAL MEDIA AMPLIFICATION

Reaching beyond just YouTube is a great way to build viewer velocity on your newest uploads, and also to reach new audiences on other platforms. You will likely find that your chosen subject matter will have niche online communities on other platforms that you can tap into.

Be Present within your Niche Community

For instance, if you create content about Mixed Martial Arts (MMA), you can find huge audiences online that are interested in this topic. The MMA Subreddit has over 700,000 Subscribers. There are Facebook groups with hundreds of thousands of members interested in discussing all MMA topics. On Instagram - the Hashtag *'martialarts'* has over 5.8 million posts.

This does not mean copy and paste your video URL into every forum and group you come across, but *actively* be present within your niche communities. For example if you spot a thread discussing the best technique to throw a roundhouse kick, this could be the perfect opportunity for you to share your video showing how to throw a sweet body kick. This is more likely to generate a positive sentiment towards your content as well as giving people a reason to watch.

Share Native Content

A common mistake many new creators make is to copy and paste their YouTube URL and share it on social media. This results in lower engagement, as YouTube URLs can be suppressed in the algorithms on other social platforms.

I like to share my videos by uploading the video's thumbnail natively on social media as pictures tend to perform better. I will copy the video's URL into the post and use an emoji (usually the pointing finger emoji) to direct viewers to the link. For gaming content, I usually include a relevant hashtag and tag the game developer or publisher directly - as they might also share my post helping me to reach a larger audience.

The chart below shows the most popular social media networks by monthly active users as of 2019.[10]

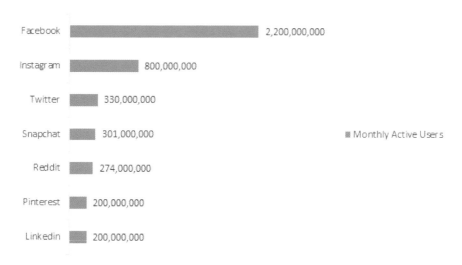

Facebook reports an estimated monthly active user base of 2.2 Billion.

Create a social media strategy to give your content the most visibility. Fostering relationships on other social media platforms will in turn help drive new fans to your YouTube content.

---

10   https://dustn.tv/social-media-statistics/

Facebook - Simply plunking your YouTube URL on Facebook might be the easiest way to share your video, however this is the least effective. Facebook tends to favour native content on the platform, so sharing just an external link is likely to only reach a small portion of your Facebook followers. Many creators have found success on Facebook by sharing an image (even a thumbnail of a video), or a section of a video can complement the Facebook algorithm to surface your post, while still driving viewers to your YouTube channel.

Instagram - Share a 30 second teaser from your video or upload a Story to announce your latest upload. Include a hook to encourage your viewers to click-through and watch the video on YouTube.

Twitter - Tweets including native video attract 10X more engagement than tweets without video.[11]. Share the YouTube URL along with accompanying text and an image or short video clip to create a more sharable Tweet. If applicable, include a relevant hashtag and tag any companies featured in the video, as they may be compelled to share the video exposing you to their audience.

Reddit - Reddit is comprised of subreddits which are subsidiary threads or categories within the Reddit website. Find appropriate subreddits to share your videos. Be mindful of any subreddit guidelines before posting.

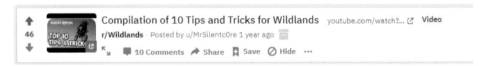

The Reddit community can quickly shoot down any shared content that does not meet their rules. Only share your content if you believe the video offers value to the subreddit community.

---

11   https://business.twitter.com/en/blog/twitter-tips_-5-ways-to-use-video-in-your-holiday-marketing-camp.html?utm_medium=organic&utm_source=twitter

Some subreddits ban 'self-promotion' to prevent people sharing their own videos - in which case you could ask a friend to share the video!

Experiment

Do not be afraid to try new social media networks as they emerge. Depending on the type of content you are creating, you may find success on certain social media platforms where your target audience is stronger.

FOSTER A POSITIVE COMMUNITY

As a YouTuber, you ultimately set the tone for your community, so be sure to lead with a good example. If your comment section is a pool of toxicity with harassment or hateful content, this will reflect poorly on you as a creator. New viewers may be deterred from subscribing and most brands will certainly stay clear, as they will not want their brand associated with such negativity.

If you find a negative comment on a video you have a few options:

- **Redirect:** If the comment is negative, first consider if you can redirect the comment into a more positive conversation. The tone and manner in which you respond to these comments can turn the conversation around into a positive mood.

- **Remove:** Manually delete the comment that also removes all replies in the thread under that comment.

- **Report:** If the comment violates YouTube's Community Guidelines you can anonymously flag the comment for YouTube by marking it as spam or abuse.

- **Hide from channel:** If the user is a repeat offender, you can use the 'Hide user from channel' option to permanently block a user from posting any further comments. I personally love this feature as the user will not be alerted that they have been hidden, so if they continue to post comments no one will ever see them!

Since most creators are not online 24/7 to moderate comments, fortunately YouTube provides you with several tools to help stay on top of community management.

PERSISTENCE AND SUSTAINABILITY

One question I am asked time and time again is: *'How do you get the motivation to keep going?'*

My answer is always - **Persistence**.

One of the best pieces of YouTube advice I have ever followed is **Just Keep Uploading**.

Now this might sound incredibly simple (because it is), but it is easily forgotten when what you want to achieve seems too far off or unattainable. But this advice works no matter what you want to achieve in life.

For example, if you want to be great at playing guitar or join a band, then you just keep practising.

If you want to be great at boxing? You just keep boxing.

If you want to be a computer programmer? You just keep programming.

It is easy to get consumed with the numbers, and even become demotivated when your content is not receiving the attention you hoped or expected. It took me a whole year of making YouTube videos to even reach my first 1,000 Subscribers! Pewdiepie, one of the most well-known personalities on YouTube, started off making small time Call of Duty videos until he found success in another niche, propelling him on the platform.

The Importance of Passion

The truth is, maintaining a successful YouTube channel is not easy, and if it was, then *everyone* would be doing it. Being a YouTuber is more of a way of life than it is a hobby. If you have a real passion for creating content and your subject matter, let that be your motivation to progress, rather than the numbers. My channel has always had a focus around video games, because I genuinely love to play them and share my experiences with them. I believe my subscribers watch my content because they can see I clearly love what I do and I make sure that comes across in my videos.

Focus on improving your content production and quality with each video you post. Join communities and networks of friends who also create content and motivate each other to keep posting. I allow creating content be my both my healthy addiction and obsession. I genuinely love creating videos and would still do it even as an unpaid hobby.

Sustainability

Creating content can be very time consuming. Ensure you have the time and resources to maintain your content schedule on a long-term basis. Many of the most successful daily vloggers such as *Life of Tom* have been posting on a daily basis without missing a day for consecutive years. They have reached sustainability by ensuring they have the time to film, edit and post a new video every day.

Being able to record multiple videos in one sitting, also known as **block shooting**, will save time, money and resources. If you have a shared YouTube channel, are the other contributors able to commit as much time and energy into maintaining the channel as you are?

Sustainability also includes your personal energy. If a video absorbs a huge amount of your time and energy, you may want to reconsider the concept to create a more sustainable series. Are you creating content from your genuine interest in the topic? Otherwise your audience will know and you are more likely to get burnt out.

Health and well-being

Being a YouTube creator for most people is far from a traditional 9 to 5 job. I tend to spend *a lot* of time at the computer every day, so I make a conscious effort not to get sucked into my mobile phone too much when I am out. Even on holidays, I still find myself thinking about YouTube and anxious about whether my views will diminish on my return.

Keeping a healthy body and a happy mind should always be your number one priority. If you are constantly stressed or exhausted by your workflow, this will take a toll on your body and start to negatively influence your content. Taking time offline to recharge will help you feel refreshed and motivated to create content.

Here are some ways to maintain a YouTube/Life Balance:

- **Time management:** Get a planner or journal to schedule time to work and time for yourself.

- **Fresh air:** Get outside in sunshine for at least 30 minutes per day to get adequate Vitamin D (this can be easier said than done if you are from Scotland like myself!).

- **Exercise regularly:** Hitting the gym or finding a sport you enjoy is a great reason to leave the house and de-stress.

- **Eat healthy:** It should go without saying that avoiding overly processed foods will improve your health and contribute to how your body feels.

- **Get enough sleep:** If you are not getting enough sleep each night your energy levels will suffer and affect your motivation to create content.

- **Holidays:** Taking vacations will help avoid burnout from creating content 24/7. You can use YouTube's video scheduler to plan ahead or consider letting your audience know you will be taking a break, as viewers are generally understanding.

- **Privacy:** You do not need to share *everything* with your fans. Keeping full names, home addresses and license plates hidden in your content is a good idea.

- **Happiness:** Disassociate happiness with the performance of your channel. Find external factors that positively influence your mood.

CHAPTER 3 CHECKLIST

The key to growing an active audience on YouTube is to maintain momentum. With no momentum, your audience will likely forget about you. Use this checklist to follow some of the best strategies to build momentum.

- [ ] *Create high quality videos. This should always be your first goal*

- [ ] *Convert as many viewers to subscribers as possible*

- [ ] *Regularly interact with your audience, even when you are not uploading*

- [ ] *Set an upload schedule*

- [ ] *Collaborate and cross-promote with other creators*

- [ ] *Seek local networking opportunities*

- [ ] *Amplify your videos on social media*

CHAPTER 4

ANALYTICS

As a YouTube creator, understanding the YouTube analytics dashboard is the best way to statistically evaluate individual video performance or your channel's overall health. It also offers tools to understand exactly who your audience are, how they are finding you and how you can keep them watching longer. When it comes to collaborating with brands (we will be covering this in the next chapter), they are likely to ask for a copy of your channel's demographics to insure that your audience aligns with the audience they wish to target.

INCLUDED IN CHAPTER 4

- ☑ *Analytics Overview*

- ☑ *Reach Viewers*

- ☑ *Interest Viewers*

- ☑ *Build an Audience*

- ☑ *Earn Revenue*

ANALYTICS OVERVIEW

The latest YouTube Analytics dashboard is split into 5 different tabs. The first being the channel overview tab that will display key metrics for your channel's activity, including Watch Time, views, subscriber growth and estimated revenue if you are a YouTube Partner.

You can adjust the time range to compare your channel's performance for the past week, month, year, lifetime or even a custom date range.

Each section in Analytics has info cards that can be expanded by clicking on them and from here you can even download and export the full report.

How to access your channel's Analytics:

1. Sign into YouTube and visit your creator studio (https://studio.youtube.com)

2. Select Analytics from the left menu

3. Click Community and add moderators by channel URL

REACH VIEWERS

In this tab you can find your overall channel reach.

This section enables you to discover:

- How viewers find your videos on YouTube?

- What thumbnails are effective at grabbing attention?

- If you had a viral hit - where did the views come from?

Impressions, Click-through rates and unique viewers are new metrics added in early 2018. These metrics contain powerful data to give a deeper understanding of how videos perform on YouTube and their potential reach. Due to this being a new feature to analytics, YouTube has limited data before January 1st 2018.

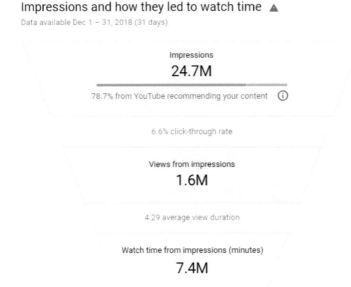

Impressions and how they led to watch time ▲
Data available Dec 1 – 31, 2018 (31 days)

Impressions
24.7M

78.7% from YouTube recommending your content ⓘ

6.6% click-through rate

Views from impressions
1.6M

4:29 average view duration

Watch time from impressions (minutes)
7.4M

24.7 million impressions is 24.7 million opportunities
to acquire a view

Impressions

Impressions are how many times your thumbnails were shown to viewers on YouTube. This allows you to see the total potential reach of your content on YouTube as each impression is an opportunity to gain a view. So if YouTube displays your video in search results or within recommended videos on the right side of the video player, this is registered as an impression.

What is **not** counted as an impression?

• The video thumbnail is shown for less than 1 second

• If less than 50% of the thumbnail is visible to the viewer

• A viewer clicks on the URL link of a video

• Views from external sources such as social media or website embeds

Impressions Click-through rate (CTR)

This is the percentage of viewers that watched a video after being shown a thumbnail. CTR measures how effective your video titles and thumbnails are to turn impressions into views. According to YouTube, half of all videos on the platform have an average CTR of 2-10%. If your CTR is at the lower end, look to optimise your video titles and thumbnails for your target audience.

Watch Time

Watch Time is the amount of time, in aggregate, that viewers spend watching your videos. Comparing impressions with CTR, you can understand how effective your video titles and thumbnails are. However, if viewers are clicking on your video but not sticking around, this will reduce your Watch Time and have a negative impact on your channel in the YouTube algorithm.

Traffic Sources

The two main traffic sources are internal sources on YouTube, and external sources, such as social media, blogs and websites. The traffic sources reports show where viewers discover your content, and how this changes over time. This enables you to see if your videos are being shared externally on social networking websites such as Facebook, or featured on popular blogs or websites.

Traffic source: YouTube search

Watch time · Last 28 days

red dead redemption 2	10.6%
red dead redemption 2 facts	1.1%
red dead redemption 2 gameplay	1.1%
red dead redemption 2 map	1.0%
red dead redemption 2 100 facts	0.5%

During the launch of video game Red Dead Redemption 2, many game related search terms were driving views to my content. I used these search terms to create even more content around popular search queries. I even turned 'Red Dead Redemption 2 Facts' into a mini-series due to the volume of search traffic for this term. You can also click on the *'Traffic Source: YouTube Search'* info box to review all the search phrases your videos are ranking for.

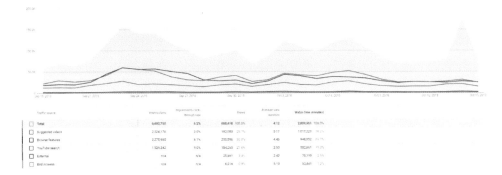

By expanding the 'Traffic Source: Types' info box, you can analyse the data by comparing how effective your video titles and thumbnails are. YouTube search and Browse features tend to have the highest Impressions CTR, as viewers have a higher intent to watch, if they are looking for specific content.

INTEREST VIEWERS

The Interest viewers tab shows what videos are being watched the most. This section displays the total Watch Time and the average view duration over time.

The average view duration measures how many of your viewers are watching all the way through your videos. Audience retention can be reviewed on a channel level or on a per-video basis. You can select a specific video by entering the video title into the search box when in the Analytics Dashboard.

Audience retention

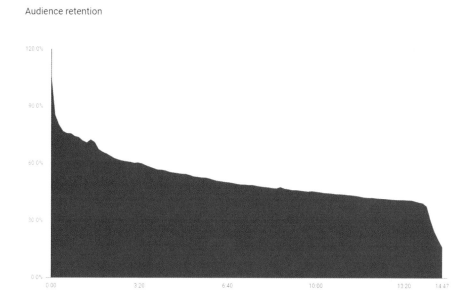

This 12 minute video had an average view duration of 7 minutes and 22 seconds. My viewers on average are watching 58.2% of the video before leaving

It is completely normal to have some audience drop-off at the start of a video - the first 15 seconds is when viewers are most likely to drop-off. A good average retention rate is at least 50-60%. The closer you can get to 100% viewer retention, the better!

Figure A on the left is an example of a **bad** audience retention report. The graph shows a large audience drop-off from the beginning of the video, indicating that the video was not what the viewers expected from the title and thumbnail.

Figure B on the right portrays a more **irregular** audience retention. Dips show the exact points where viewers skip ahead or are leaving the video. Rising peaks indicate areas where viewers are re-watching or even sharing the video with a later starting point.

Low audience retention can be detrimental to a video's success, as YouTube will deem the content as something viewers are not interested

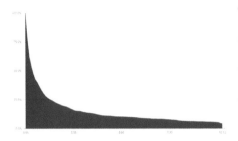

(A) This was a 10 minute video that had an average view duration of only 1 minute and 24 seconds - only 13.8% of the video!

(B) Viewer retention increases towards the video's mid-point, indicating the intro was too long, and viewers wanted to get into the content

in. This results in the YouTube algorithm punishing the video by lowering its ranking. This makes it harder for new viewers to find your content which will decrease the overall Watch Time of your channel.

Here are a few ways to increase your audience retention:

- **Shorten your introductions:** Viewers have a short attention span - If you are taking over a minute to introduce yourself or the video, you will be losing the attention of viewers.

- **Add a Hook:** Entice your viewers to keep watching by delivering a hook within the first few seconds of the video. This could be a quick recap of what the video is all about, or a short highlight clip of the video's climax to tease viewers.

- **Consolidate your video:** This is particularly important if you notice sudden spikes in your audience retention report. This indicates that viewers are skipping ahead to the part they want to watch. Consider spending more time on post-production to cut unnecessary content and make your videos more concise.

- **Constant self-promotion:** We all like to promote our merchandise, website and social media pages, but this can be jarring for viewers if done too aggressively. Either blend the call-to-actions within the content - or save it for towards the end of the video when viewers are getting ready to leave anyway.

- **Sponsorships timing:** Brands typically like to be featured at the start of a video, however this can be extremely detrimental to a video's performance, as viewers can turn away if they land on a video and are instantly being sold a product. Try to integrate the brand or product throughout the content, once viewers are already committed to the video.

BUILD AN AUDIENCE

Learning who your audience are can help you improve your content and make better creative decisions based on that data. The Demographics report breaks down exactly who is viewing your content, by viewer age, gender and geographical location.

As you grow your audience, take note of who is watching your content and compare that with your desired target audience. Keep a screenshot of this tab handy, as brands are likely to request a copy of these demographics before any potential sponsorships.

Viewer Age

In the example below, the audience is largest within the 18-24 age range, but *most* of the audience is over 25. If the ideal demographic is a younger audience - perhaps creating brighter thumbnails could attract more viewers within that age range.

Age
Watch time · Last 28 days

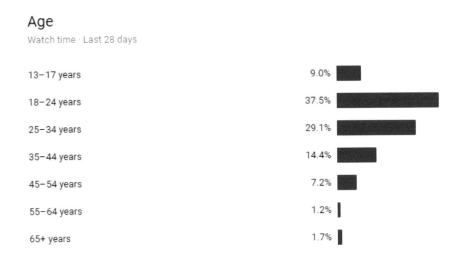

13–17 years	9.0%
18–24 years	37.5%
25–34 years	29.1%
35–44 years	14.4%
45–54 years	7.2%
55–64 years	1.2%
65+ years	1.7%

Viewer Gender

Creating gaming videos on YouTube resulted in my channel having a predominantly male audience of over 90%! Because of my channel's large gender split, I know that by creating videos geared towards males I will be reaching more of my audience.

Gender
Watch time · Last 28 days

Male	94.3%
Female	5.7%

Geography

You might be surprised to see how diverse your audience is. Only 15.6% of my viewers originate from my home country in the United Kingdom. To delve deeper into your geographics you can click on each country to see the age and gender for each country. The United States also shows a breakout of exactly which states your viewers are based in.

If you have a large viewer base in non-English speaking countries, you could consider using closed captions or translated metadata to make the content more accessible in these regions (discussed in detail in Chapter 2). Geographic data can also be used to create location-specific videos or to enable you to strategically plan what meetups or events to attend in your top countries.

Top countries
Watch time · Last 28 days

United States	44.9%
United Kingdom	15.6%
Canada	4.6%
Australia	2.9%
Netherlands	2.1%

Watch Time from Subscribers

If the bulk of your Watch Time comes from existing channel subscribers, this indicates that your videos are not reaching new audiences. Try comparing this with traffic sources to understand exactly where this Watch Time is coming from.

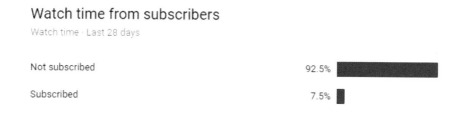

Watch time from subscribers
Watch time · Last 28 days

Not subscribed	92.5%
Subscribed	7.5%

The majority of Watch Time on my channel shows that my videos are being discovered through search and recommended features - but I need to do a better job at retaining and converting these unsubscribed viewers into subscribers.

EARN REVENUE

The last tab is exclusive for YouTube Partners and will help track and analyse your channel's monetisation. This is an important section, as you can evaluate how your audience contributes to your payments, which helps influence decisions for future videos.

The revenue report will display an overview of the different on-YouTube income streams including ad revenue, YouTube premium revenue and transaction revenue.

- **YouTube Ad Revenue:** Google-sold advertising that will be estimated until the end of month adjustment.

- **YouTube Premium Revenue:** Calculated by how much time Premium viewers spend watching your content.

- **Transaction Revenue:** Generated by transactions from YouTube purchases, channel memberships and Super chat.

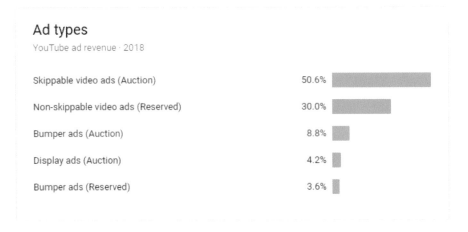

Skippable video ads make up the largest portion of my monthly revenue. These can be inserted before, during or after a video.

Understanding your CPM:

The Playback-based CPM (cost per Mille) is the estimated average gross revenue per 1,000 playbacks where an ad was shown. Since YouTube will not display an ad impression for every view - this can be compared with estimated monetised playbacks, that track how many times a viewer saw at least 1 ad while watching a video.

To calculate what you *actually* make from each 1,000 views, you need to calculate the effective CPM (or eCPM). This is because not all viewers will be served an advertisement when viewing your videos.

To calculate your eCPM, you divide your earnings, by monetised views, and then multiply the result by 1,000.

$$eCPM = \frac{Earnings}{Monetised\ views} \times 1,000$$

For example; if you received 200,000 monetised playbacks in June and earned $500 advertising revenue, your eCPM would be $2.50.

If you wanted to assess your channel's eCPM performance, it is best to compare with the same month(s) in a previous year. This will give a better comparison as advertising rates and viewership fluctuate from month to month.

How to improve your CPM

Your channel's CPM will be influenced by a variety of factors. To improve your CPM rate you need to first understand what factors influence your YouTube channel's monetisation in order to optimise them.

- **Content Category:** Brands use content categories to target specific audiences and interests. CPM rates tend to vary across content categories as advertiser spends fluctuate. For example, creating a video discussing finance and investing may have a higher CPM than a video discussing puppies, if advertisers are spending more on ads in the finance sector. (*Note: this is a fictional example, I do not know how the ad rates between puppies and finance compare!*)

- **Macro-Trends:** Current global economic conditions can impact ad rates globally.

- **Seasonality:** Advertising spend tends to vary throughout the year. Advertisers tend to spend more money at the end of the year than they do at the start of the year. So do not be surprised if your CPM drastically drops from December into January! If you are launching a new YouTube series, you could try timing it when advertisers tend to spend more money such as during holidays or towards the end of a financial quarter.

- **Geographical Location:** YouTube has a global audience but ad rates vary from region to region. For example, a channel primarily for a US based audience is likely to have a higher CPM than a channel primarily for an audience in Mexico, which has a less developed advertising market. Some countries are completely ineligible for ads, as advertisers can only target ads in countries where YouTube has launched a monetised website (see YouTube's Monetised Markets[12] for an updated list). Strive to reach more viewers in monetised markets that pay out at a higher CPM.

- **Enabled Ad-formats:** Each ad type will earn at a different CPM. Advertisers will pay a high CPM for non-skippable video ads, compared with very low rates for Display ads.

- **Devices:** What device viewers are watching on will affect how ads are monetised. For example, views on mobile devices are lower than other devices as not all ad formats are available on mobile.

---

12   https://support.google.com/youtube/answer/1342206

- **Brand Friendly:** Most advertisers prefer to run ads alongside content that follows YouTube's advertiser-friendly guidelines. Some creators have found that swearing within a video has more than halved their CPM rate on that video! A video can also be completely restricted from monetisation if it does not comply with YouTube's terms.

- **Watch-time:** Creating great content is the foundation to increase monetisable playbacks and CPM. The more your audience grows and engages with your videos, the more attractive you will be to advertisers.

CHAPTER 4 CHECKLIST

In order to make the most out of your YouTube channel, you can use YouTube Analytics to track metrics to help improve the performance of your videos. Here is a checklist of metrics worth tracking to achieve long-term success on YouTube.

- ☐ *Check how impressions relate to Watch Time*

- ☐ *Track your Subscriber Growth Rate*

- ☐ *Check the click-through rates for Cards and End Screens*

- ☐ *Study your likes to dislikes*

- ☐ *Identify your biggest Traffic Sources*

- ☐ *Analyse Audience Retention Reports*

- ☐ *Determine your Audience Demographics to understand your viewers*

- ☐ *Compare your CPM rate across different types of videos to see what monetises best*

MONETISATION

YouTube announced that in 2018, the number of creators earning 5 figures increased by 35% and the number of creators earning over six-figures increased by a whopping 45%.[13] And these numbers represent only the advertising revenue generated on YouTube and not from other external sources.

Monetisation is an important aspect of being a YouTube creator. Not only can you make money (because who doesn't like money right?), but it enables many people to focus on creating videos as their full time career. If your videos cost money to produce, monetisation is required for you to establish a sustainable business.

13   https://youtube-creators.googleblog.com/2018/04/an-update-on-our-2018-priorities.html

INCLUDED IN CHAPTER 5

☑ *On and off-site Sources of Revenue*

☑ *YouTube Partnership Program*

☑ *Types of branded sponsorships*

☑ *How to get more brand deals*

☑ *Pricing your channel*

☑ *Prohibited advertisements*

☑ *Disclosures*

SOURCES OF REVENUE

When it comes to monetising a YouTube channel - there are a variety of on and off-site options. Each source of revenue is called a revenue stream - and you want as many revenue streams as possible, to avoid being reliant on just one.

On-site Monetisation:

- YouTube Advertising Revenue
- Super Chat
- Monthly Channel Memberships (*Previously: Sponsorship Button*)

Off-site Monetisation:

- Merchandise
- Crowdfunding
- Event appearances
- Affiliate sponsorships
- Product sponsorships
- Paid sponsorships

YOUTUBE ADVERTISING REVENUE

To enable your YouTube videos for monetisation and earn a portion of advertising revenue, you must first join the YouTube Partnership Program.

The partner program has gone through several major changes over the years; from being very exclusive, to allowing anyone to monetise their videos, and more recently to tightening the YouTube partner program requirements again. The good news is that the partner program requirements are still relatively low, so you will not missing out much advertising revenue from being under the threshold.

YouTube Partnership Program

First of all, you will need to create an AdSense account or connect an existing AdSense account to your YouTube account to receive payments

YouTube Partner Program Requirements:

- You must reside in a country where the partner program is available
- You must have 1,000 subscribers, minimum
- You must have had 4,000 hours of Watch Time within the last 12 months

How to apply to join the YouTube Partner Program:

1. Sign into YouTube and visit your creator studio (https://studio.youtube.com)
2. Click Channel, then Status and Features
3. Click the Monetisation section to enable channel Monetisation (or visit this page directly https://www.youtube.com/account_monetization)

When you reach the threshold requirements, YouTube will manually review your channel to ensure you abide by all the YouTube Community Guidelines, Partner Policies and Terms of Service. The length of time it takes YouTube to review your channel after you meet the requirements, depends on the number of pending applications at the time you apply. YouTube have confirmed they prioritise larger channels receiving more views - so if you have a larger channel your channel will be reviewed quicker.

Understanding the YouTube Ecosystem

The YouTube ecosystem is a real-time loop that relies on three groups: viewers, creators and advertisers. It is essential that all 3 groups are satisfied and working in synergy for optimum performance of the YouTube ecosystem.

Viewers - YouTube should be the best place for viewers to discover and view content online.

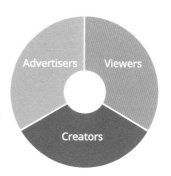

Creators - YouTube should be the best place to post content that viewers want to watch, while making a source of revenue.

Advertisers - YouTube should be a platform that enables advertisers to reach their target audiences. This in turn funds creators who expose their ads.

Advertising on YouTube comes in several different formats. To maximise your revenue you should always enable all types of ads. You can do this by checking all of the ad types in the monetisation settings of each video you upload.

If your video is longer than 10 minutes in length, you can enable additional ads to be placed during the middle of a video.
If you ever wondered why so many videos on YouTube are 10:05 in length - this is likely why!

YouTube ad formats include:

- **Display ads:** These ads appear alongside your video to viewers watching on desktop computers. Display ads offer low revenue rates, but you will receive revenue for viewers that *click* on the ad and also for those that *see* your ad, (these are called *impressions*).

- **Overlay ads:** This banner appears over the video on desktop computers A viewer can either click to expand the ad or click the X in the top right corner of the banner to close the ad. As a creator you need to be mindful of these ads, as they can cover the lower 20% of your video. Keep this in mind when editing, as any text at the start of a video, in the lower quadrant of the screen, may be covered if an overlay ad is displayed!

- **Sponsored Cards:** In the same way you can insert your own cards in videos, YouTube can display cards that display relevant products. Viewers on desktop and mobile devices will see the card pop up in the top right corner of the video

- **Skippable video ads:** This is the most popular ad format available on all viewing devices, from desktop, to mobile, to game consoles. Video ads can be inserted before the video starts, during the video, or after the video has finished. Viewers can skip the video ad after watching the first 5 seconds.

- **Bumper ads:** These are non-skippable video ads that last up to 6 seconds. Viewers on desktop and mobile devices are shown this ad before the video begins.

- **Mid-roll ads:** If your video is over 10 minutes in length, you unlock the ability to add mid-roll ads for desktop and mobile viewers. You can allow YouTube to automatically insert them, or manually splice these into your videos and strategically choose a placement within your video that will encourage viewers to watch the ad, and then continue watching your video. Although you could cram the video full of mid-roll ads, thinking you will make a ton of money - this is likely to actually drive viewers away from your video. If the video is just over 10 minutes long, inserting an ad halfway at the 5-6 minute mark would be preferable. If your video is longer, such as over 30 minutes you can potentially add several mid-rolls spaced throughout. Consider the optimal viewer experience - especially for your regular viewers.

Being Advertiser Friendly

To be suitable for advertising, your video must abide by **YouTube's Advertiser-friendly content guidelines**. As a YouTube Partner you can still upload videos that are not completely advertiser-friendly - however you should always manually turn off monetisation on these videos. If you do try to monetise videos that break the advertiser-friendly guidelines, you risk losing access to future monetisation.

YouTube takes into consideration your thumbnail, video title, description, tags and the actual content of your video to determine if it is advertiser-friendly. Be mindful when entering tags that certain keywords can trigger the video to automatically be deemed unsafe and result in no ads being shown until the video has been manually reviewed by YouTube.

Here is a list of YouTube's advertiser-friendly guidelines on content that can result in your videos receiving limited or no ads whatsoever:

- **Controversial issues and sensitive events:** Any videos discussing sensitive topics such as war, tragedies or abuse.

- **Drugs and dangerous products or substances:** Featuring any dangerous substances or using illegal drugs.

- **Harmful or dangerous acts:** Promoting physical or emotional injuries, or even pranks involving harassment or humiliation.

- **Hateful content:** This can include humiliating an individual or discrimination against groups.

- **Inappropriate language:** Frequent use of profanity or strong language can flag your video as not suitable for advertising.

- **Inappropriate use of family entertainment characters:** This one is pretty self-explanatory.

- **Incendiary and demeaning:** Creating an inflammatory video that shames or insults an individual or group.

- **Sexually suggestive content:** If the video topic is highly sexualised or if any nudity is shown throughout the video.

- **Violence:** This one can be a grey area, especially when video game footage is involved. In many video games violence is considered a normal aspect of the game. However, if the focal point of your video is involving blood or violence such as my montage of Mortal Kombat X Fatalities, then it may not be suitable for advertisers!

Of course context *does* matter. It can be difficult for an algorithm to detect the context of your video so thankfully YouTube does offer the ability to appeal the decision and have it reviewed by a real person. For example, if your video mentions a weapon or drug substance for educational or documentary purposes - your video may be eligible for advertising.

You can check the monetisation status of your content in your video manager. Monetised videos will be marked with a green dollar symbol, whereas videos not suitable for advertisers will be marked with a yellow dollar symbol (every YouTuber's worst nightmare). Within the video manager, you can click to view videos that have 'Limited or no ads' to quickly identify any videos you need to review.

If your video does indeed follow all the advertiser-friendly guidelines, simply click 'Request Review' and wait for a member of YouTube's review team to manually review your video. If the video was incorrectly marked as unsafe for advertisers you will receive a notice that the monetisation has been reinstated - otherwise YouTube will confirm the content is unsuitable for most advertisers.

SUPER CHAT

YouTube introduced Super Chat in January 2017 as a new way for fans to donate to creators. Built primarily for monetising live streams, viewers can donate and have their message highlighted in the chat section. Super Chats will be highlighted in a different colour from normal messages and stay pinned for a period of time giving the donator greater exposure for their contribution. The higher the dollar amount of the donation - the longer the comment will be pinned.

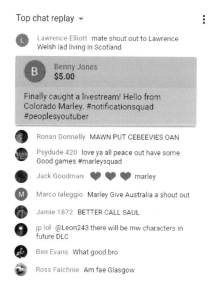

Marleythirteen regularly live streams himself playing Call of Duty and his viewers frequently send Super Chat donations to ask questions or simply as a show of support.

YouTube takes a hefty 30% cut of any Super Chat donations. Apple may also take a cut if the Super Chat is sent via iOS. However Super Chats do offer the ease of accessibility and security, as the donations are made directly through the YouTube platform. This avoids driving viewers to a third-party service to make a donation. Creators also do not need to worry about potential chargebacks and refunds that can occur on other platforms.

Super Chat Requirements:

- 1,000 subscribers minimum
- You are over the age of 18
- You must reside in a an eligible country
- You must be in the YouTube Partner Program

MONTHLY CHANNEL MEMBERSHIPS

Channel memberships (*previously "Channel Sponsorships"*) allow viewers to make monthly payments to support your channel. YouTube will retain a 30% cut of all channel membership revenue. However, YouTube will cover any transaction costs and credit card fees associated with these payments.

Creators can offer benefits known as 'perks' exclusively to Channel Members. These benefits include a custom badge that appears next to comments made by Channel Members and access to custom emojis.

Having great emojis, that your fans love to use, can be a big incentive for converting viewers into members. You can use marketplaces such as Fiverr to find very affordable graphic designers who specialise in creating graphics for YouTubers (Feel free to use my referral for 20% off your first order http://bit.ly/fiverrdiscount).

CA$4.99/month

JOIN

Recurring payment. Cancel anytime.
Creator may update perks from time to time. Learn more

- Exclusive access to loyalty badges in comments and live chat

- Custom Emojis
  Access to custom emojis

- Custom Chat Badge
  Custom chat badge next to your name when you comment on my channel

Making a video to announce when channel memberships are live on your channel can be a fantastic way to kick-start a new feature. Take time to explain why you have channel memberships, how it helps support your channel and get your fans excited about the perks! You can also give a verbal mention to new channel members who join your channel within your videos to personally thank them.

Channel Memberships Requirements:

- 30,000 subscribers minimum

- You are over the age of 18

- You must reside in a an eligible country

- Be in the YouTube Partner Program

- Channel enabled for live streaming

- Currently only "gaming" channels are eligible

MULTI-CHANNEL NETWORKS (MCNS)

As your channel grows on YouTube it is likely you will receive offers from third-party Multi-Channel Networks (or MCNs as they are commonly known). I often get as many as several offers per week!

These networks are not officially endorsed by YouTube or Google, and there is no real *need* to sign with one, unless it will add substantial value to your channel. You can find thousands of MCNs out there waiting to sign creators under their umbrella, all with varying amounts of value. This can come with benefits such as: promotion, collaborations, channel development, copyright management and sometimes, additional monetisation opportunities. However, this does come at a price, typically a cut of your channel's advertising revenue. I have seen networks offering to take anything from 5% to 60% of a channel's revenue! Depending how many views your channel is receiving - this can be a huge amount of money to forfeit.

Keep in mind that MCN offerings can look very attractive on paper, such as having a 1 on 1 channel manager who will help increase your channel's views and revenue. However, many of the large networks have over 50,000 YouTube partners in their content management systems - which as you can imagine would be a huge task to attend to the needs of each individual channel.

If you do consider any agreements with a MCN, it is always best to have a lawyer review the contract, as it is legally binding. One of my first contracts was actually 'perpetual' - which means forever! Always check the termination clause, and how long the contract will be. Shorter contract terms are usually better, so if the network does not provide value, you are not tied down for a long period of time.

MERCHANDISE

When used correctly, merchandise and sales can become a large income stream for your business. When most people think about merchandise, they think of t-shirts, but you can go beyond this and offer products relevant to your channel's content. Or even sell books like this one!

What Merchandise should you offer?

The first step is to research your target audience and consider what products they are likely to want or better yet - actually need. For example, if you run a child care channel aimed towards mothers raising children, they probably aren't going to want snapback hats.

A great example of targeted merchandise is the YouTube channel 'Clean my Space' - a channel dedicated to providing the best content on cleaning. They released their own microfiber cleaning towel that is not only relevant to their target audience, but something the audience are  likely to need, since they are watching cleaning related videos. Melissa Maker, the host and owner of the Clean my Space channel is also able to mention and feature the product in many videos in an authentic way.

Reinforce your brand:

Does your channel have strong branding? A well designed logo can look great on general merchandise, from clothing to accessories such as phone cases, and will reinforce your brand. If your channel incorporates any other key themes also consider including them into your designs. Popular YouTube personality Jenna Marbles uses her dogs, who regularly feature in her videos on her merchandise items.

If you have any regular catch-phrases you use on your channel, this can also be a great way to make your merchandise extra special for your audience. Fellow Scottish YouTuber *Batchy* created a t-shirt with the quote *'Get oot ma hoose'* (Translated: "Get out my house" for anyone not from Scotland!). Although the quote does not necessarily represent Batchy's channel to an outsider, it is a quote regularly used within his content and gives a special way to involve his regular viewers with an inside joke.

Distribution:

Managing orders, printing and shipping can be a very time consuming process. Make sure your products are easy to deliver and cost-efficient to make. As your channel grows you are likely to be bombarded with merchandise opportunities from companies looking to handle the distribution for your products - for a cut of the pie obviously. This can be helpful if you simply want to create a design and have someone else take care of the logistics.

My recommendation when working with distributors is to check the quality of their products. If the t-shirts are made cheaply and lose their designs after a few washes - your fans will not be impressed and will be unlikely to purchase more. Ask for product samples and make sure it is a product you are happy using yourself, and having your name associated with before your start promoting it.

YouTube has a list of approved third party merchandise distributors[14] that you can refer to within your videos using cards and end screens.

---

14   https://support.google.com/youtube/answer/6083754

- **Create relevant products:** Make sure your merchandise and designs are something that your audience will actually want.

- **Involve your community**: Get your community excited about the launches of each product, and let them know how much their purchases help support your channel.

- **Integrate your merchandise into your content:** Find ways to regularly expose your audience to your merchandise.

- **Limited edition products**: Try creating a product that is only available for a short period of time, this gives your hardcore fans an opportunity to own something exclusive, that no one else can get. Having time-limited offers is a great way to incentive your audience to make a purchase, rather than having an infinite amount of time to purchase a product that is always available

- **Promote your buyers:** Encourage your audience to share images of your products on social media. This will not only help to get the word out about your merchandise, but you can also share these images on your own social media and videos as testimonials. Your fans are also likely to love being highlighted on your social media or videos!

- **Source inspiration from your fans**: Ask your audience what kinds of merchandise they would like! Perhaps even run a design competition for your audience to create designs for an upcoming product.

CROWDFUNDING

Crowdfunding allows your fans to contribute money towards a project or to help financially support your YouTube channel. This gives you more freedom to create and experiment, without having to worry about getting income from ad revenue alone. Even for small to medium sized creators, crowdfunding from your audience can help fund your next big idea, or open up a new revenue stream that enables you to start creating content on YouTube *full time*.

If your videos have high production costs, such as writers, editors, equipment and a studio space - this could be subsidised by having your audience directly support the content you are making. Even small to medium sized creators working from home can benefit from crowdfunding by having their audience contribute to software or equipment costs to produce videos. You may be surprised by the generosity of your audience who love your videos and want to actively take a part in supporting your channel to the next level.

One of the biggest barriers I see from creators starting a crowdfunding page - are concerns about how their audience will react. After all it is always awkward having to ask people for money. However, crowdfunding is generally well received by YouTube audiences if the creator is honest and transparent on why they are doing it and why it will benefit their audience.

You do not need to have a huge channel to start crowdfunding, but you do need to have some engaged viewers. The subscribers that watch all of your videos and leave comments and likes on the video are more likely to support your channel than passive viewers. If your audience is requesting you to post more content - they may be willing to contribute to your crowdfunding campaign in order to get more content from you.

Project-Based Crowdfunding:

The two main types of crowdfunding are project based, and recurring. Project based is a one-off campaign to fund a specific project or goal such as a professional DSLR camera, a large ambitious video idea, creating a product or even developing your own game or app. Parts of project based crowdfunding can also be used to raise money for charities.

Project based crowdfunding is also a great way to have your audience assist with expensive equipment. For a small creator this could be a goal of $200 to purchase a professional microphone to improve the audio quality of all future videos. Regular viewers will have the increased incentive of financially supporting this goal as they would get more value out of your future videos with the increased quality.

Recurring Crowdfunding:

Recurring crowdfunding is when sponsors choose to make regular donations. This can be a donation per video, or a subscription to make a monthly donation. Say you have 10,000 subscribers, if only 1% of your audience pledges to donate just $5 per month, that's an extra $500 every month. If you have 100,000 subscribers, and again 1% of your audience sponsors your channel with $5 per month, that's an additional $5,000 monthly income!

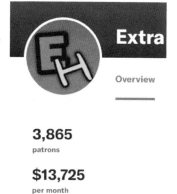

Setting a great example of recurring crowdfunding is *Extra History* who creates educational high-quality animated shorts. They have accumulated a large community of patrons pledging over $13,000 per month! By crowdfunding, *Extra History* have been able to invest in improving the quality of their video animations, and hiring additional staff to increase the quantity of videos released every week. The donors also have a set of unique rewards, depending how much they contribute every month. These rewards range from early access to videos, to even having their name listed in the credits of their videos.

Tiered Rewards

Both project-based and recurring crowdfunders can make use of tiered rewards to further incentive viewers to contribute and even contribute more than originally intended in order to reach a certain reward. Make sure your rewards are rewarding and sustainable, and will not become too time consuming to fulfil - otherwise this may impact on your content schedule.

Example Recurring Reward Structure:

- $1 per month - Access to exclusive patron-only chat group

- $5 per month - 1 day early access to videos

- $10 per month - Monthly patron only hangout or livestream

- $50 per month - Names listed as contributors within each video

When it comes to actually creating your crowdfunder, it is important to take the time to choose the right platform. YouTube has an extensive list of approved third-party crowdfunding websites that you can link to within your YouTube videos using cards and end screens. Some crowdfunding platforms may only allow either project-based campaigns or recurring campaigns, with varying amounts of customisation for rewards and of course the terms and conditions for how fees are managed.

BEST-PRACTICES:

- Decide what crowdfunding campaign **best suits your goal** - is it a one-off project based or something that requires the regular support of a recurring campaign?

- Define a dollar amount as an **overall goal and what reaching that goal will mean**. For a musician this could be a goal of $2,000 per month to release a new song that sponsors will get to hear early.

- **Design a tiered structure for your patrons with rewards** depending how much they contribute. This could include early access to videos, stickers (that can be shipped cheaply), monthly Q&A hangouts, behind the scenes of your video or even a patron only email list or chat group where your supporters can chat to you directly.

- Make your goals **relative to the size of your channel**. If you create a goal way too high then you may discourage some people from donating, as they will see it as unobtainable. Refer to similar crowdfunded campaigns and similar YouTube channels to get some idea of how much money you can raise through crowdfunding.

- Create a video to **announce your crowdfunding campaign**. Be honest and upfront with your audience. Why do you need their support? How will their support benefit your channel and give them more value as a viewer?

- **Maintain momentum** by regularly promoting the crowdfunding campaign and updating your audience on how close you are to reaching your goal.

- **Thank your patrons** - always show your gratitude for the support from your audience and show what goals you have reached as a result of their support.

EVENT APPEARANCES

Seek out local events, conferences, industry mixers and networking summits related to your subject field. If your YouTube channel is focused on winter sports - are there any Ski or Snowboard events scheduled in your local area? Event organisers are usually very easy to contact and always looking for marketing opportunities to sell more tickets for their events.

 Special Guest Appearances can be a tricky one to price as it varies greatly depending on the event and industry you are creating content around. Some events will schedule special guests to appear at official meet and greets, panels, audience Q&A (question and answer) sessions and workshops.

Consider what a day of your time is worth, how much money you could have otherwise generated from that day that you would be missing out on. For example: Could you create 3 videos in a day that would otherwise generate you £500? Would you need to use an unpaid vacation day from your day job to attend the event? These should all be factored into your asking price.

If attending the event also requires additional deliverables, such as social media posts, or a video on your channel announcing your presence at the event, then this should also be added to your overall fee for attending the event.

If the event does not offer any budget for special guests, another avenue for remuneration is to work with the event exhibitors. Many events will sell booth space for brands that wish to exhibit their products to attending consumers. The pricing varies from show to show but exhibitors will be paying anything from several hundred dollars to hundreds of thousands of dollars to exhibit at major events. Brands are willing to pay the high costs of exhibiting in order to reach the attending audiences. Since they are already spending marketing budget to attend the event, you can amplify their presence at the event through your online reach and influence.

The most common forms of brand amplification at events are social media posts, showcasing the brand and their booth location at the event, and even small 'meet and greet' gatherings at the brand's exhibiting booth - where you announce a time you will be there to meet fans, sign things and take pictures. The brand will also be happy to see their booth and logo visible in the background of all the pictures your fans will be sharing online.

BEST PRACTICES:

- **Reach out to events** you are interested in attending to start a conversation. Begin by introducing yourself, your channel and why you would like to attend.

- Outline how you could **provide value to the event** such as producing a video vlog or experience of the event, providing social media coverage or contributing to panels. This is a great way to get free tickets to events and even have your travel and accommodation provided.

- Print **business cards** to hand out at events.
- Always take the time at events to find the organiser who arranged your free tickets and **thank them for the opportunity**. This is a great way to make a first impression and increases your chances of being included in future events.

TYPES OF BRANDED SPONSORSHIPS

Influencer Marketing is a rapidly growing industry with a marketing spend of over one billion dollars[15] (and growing!). Another study[16] found that brands using influencers were able to deliver a Return on Investment (ROI) eleven times greater than traditional digital advertising, illustrating the value of brands collaborating with creators.

For new creators, working with brands can be a daunting experience. I see many creators postponing collaborations with brands as they do not believe their channel is large enough to appeal to potential advertisers. While there is no strict size requirement to work with a brand, opportunities still exist for channels with as little as 1,000 subscribers!

If brands are in tune with influencer marketing they will be looking at more than just your subscriber count. The average views per video and engagement rate are the two best metrics for them to assess. If your viewers are engaging well with your content, then they are more likely

---

15   http://mediakix.com/2018/03/influencer-marketing-indus-try-ad-spend-chart/

16   https://www.tapinfluence.com/influencer-marketing-statistics/

to engage with any brands or products featured in your videos. Brands may also request a copy of your YouTube channel's demographics report to ensure you fit within their target audience. The most common requests are where your audience is geographically located, the age of your audience, and viewer gender.

There are 3 main types of sponsorships

1. **Affiliate sponsorships**: Earn commission from sales

2. **Product sponsorships**: Receive free products

3. **Paid sponsorships**: Branded content or paid endorsements

Affiliate Sponsorships

Affiliate sponsorships are the easiest to obtain, however they are usually the least profitable form of branded collaboration. As a brand affiliate, you will be provided with your own affiliate link or a coupon code that will generate a small percentage of revenue for you each time a sale is generated through your link or code. Most affiliate programs will also have a website you can login to and track how many visitors and sales you have generated.

I have found coupon codes generally work best, as they will give your audience a discount on the product, thus giving more incentive for your viewers to make a purchase. For example as an *INTO THE AM* affiliate, I am able to give viewers 10% off any clothing purchases with my discount code 'SILENT'. Keep your coupon code short, memorable and consistent across all of your affiliates.

Affiliate links can provide long-term passive income, especially if you link them within the description of all your videos. For instance, do you have a favourite pair of headphones you wear in all your videos? Add a note in your video descriptions with an affiliate link to make it easy for viewers to purchase them.

A great affiliate program to get started with is Amazon (https://affiliate-program.amazon.com/). You can find pretty much every product under the sun listed on Amazon and generate a tracked affiliate link. Amazon is also a name people can trust, so you would be directing your viewers to a website they likely to be already familiar with. You can earn up to 10% of fees depending on what category of product you are selling. With Amazon being the most popular internet retailer in the world, you are missing out on revenue if you are recommending products within your videos and not using affiliate links.

Although the revenue generated from affiliate sponsorships are generally a small percentage, it can be a great way to open the door to future opportunities with brands. As an affiliate, there are typically less requirements (if any) from the brand on how often you need to mention the products. This means you do not have to worry about coming across as a salesman!

Product Sponsorships

The next level of branded collaborations are product sponsorships. Have I mentioned I love free stuff?

This usually involves a brand sending you free products in return for a review video or exposure within your videos or social media. Or occasionally, a company may simply want user feedback from an influencer on a product. Most product sponsorships will not have a formal contract unless it is a longer-term partnership or the product has a significant dollar value, such as a laptop or games console.

Once your content is reaching on average 1,000-10,000 views per video, your channel should be in a good position to start acquiring free products. Product sponsorships can also be accompanied with an affiliate link or coupon code unique for your audience to allow you to be compensated for sales generated from featuring any products on your channel.

SilentcOre
@SilentcOre

Want to say a huge thanks to @XboxCanada for upgrading me! All my Red Dead Redemption 2 videos so far have been recorded on the Xbox One X! 🎮
If you want to join my Xbox Crew for Red Dead Online drop your GamerTag 🐃 #RDR2 🐎

If you have a review or technology based YouTube channel, you are likely to receive the most product sponsorship offers, as products easily fit into your content format. Many hardware YouTube channels start off by purchasing their own products to review, and once they start growing an active audience they are able to receive almost everything they review for free. *ClickTech UK* is an upcoming technology channel with 2,600 subscribers. With a small dedicated audience, he receives product sponsorships on a weekly basis. He is able to offer brands a positive experience by producing dedicated videos unboxing and reviewing the products on his channel. Brands regularly provide him with additional units to giveaway to his fans, which in turn helps grow his audience.

Product sponsorships can also come in the form of more official partnerships. Partnerships may involve a formal contract or terms and conditions that restrict you working with a brand's competitors. During a product partnership with Lenovo I received several gaming laptops to giveaway and use within my videos - this involved agreeing not work with any other laptop manufacturers during the contract term.

I see many large creators turning down product sponsorships if the brand does not also throw in an additional flat fee payment. While accepting free products will not pay your rent and bills, requesting a payment on top of a product can mean completely forfeiting the opportunity. Many brands and agencies only allocate PR units (Free products distributed for Public Relations) to influencers and simply do not allocate any budget for extra payments.

Consider the value and exclusivity of the products - if you are being sent a £10 pair of headphones, they have a much lower value, in terms of promotion, than a £10,000 high-spec gaming computer to review. I would be much more inclined to make a dedicated video showcasing an awesome product that has a high value.

Are you being provided a product or game early, before it is officially released to the public? If your review has exclusivity, it will increase the chances of the video growing organically, raising the value of the opportunity.

Paid Sponsorships

The third level of sponsorships are one of the highest forms of brand content. The deliverables of each sponsorship will vary greatly depending on the brand and products you are working with, and also the size and influence of your channel. Paid sponsorships should involve a signed contract that specifies the terms and conditions and obligations required in order to receive payment.

Paid sponsorships are harder to obtain for smaller channels, as brands usually have a budget based on forecasted views. Most brands look for at least 10,000 average views per video. Of course, if you have a larger presence on other social media platforms that may also be taken into account and amplify your reach.

One of my favourite paid sponsorships was a brand deal with Samsung. I was sent a high-speed SSD to upgrade my computer and offered an additional payment for creating a dedicated video!

Paid sponsorships generally fit into one of three different categories:

1. **Branded integrations** – Sponsored integrations are one of the least intrusive forms of brand deals. This is when a sponsored segment is integrated within one of your normal, scheduled videos. The length of the integration and the placement within the video are usually both open to negotiation. I have included sponsored segments ranging from just 10 seconds long to 90 seconds long.

   Some brands may require the sponsored segment to appear within the first minute of your video to avoid any audience drop-off that may occur later in the video.

2. **Dedicated videos** - A dedicated video is when a new video is created entirely to incorporate a brand or product. This could be an unboxing video of the product, or even a comedy skit incorporating the brand. Dedicated videos tend to have higher payments than branded integrations, since the video is being created around the product and the brand should receive more exposure from a dedicated video.

3. **Partnerships** - These tend to be longer-term relationships with brands. Typically this involves a flat fee payment every month, in return for a certain number of deliverables. Having a fixed income stream every month from a partnership offers a guaranteed source of income that is more sustainable than relying on fluctuating advertising revenue on YouTube.

HOW TO GET MORE BRAND DEALS

1. Create a media kit

2. Make yourself easy to reach

3. Do your own reach-outs

Create A Media Kit

A media kit is basically a document containing your online resume (or CV as we say in the United Kingdom) that can be provided to brands. Creating a media kit for your YouTube channel not only gives brands a better introduction to you and your channel, but also saves you huge amounts of time in unnecessary negotiations and exchanges.

This was a quick Media Kit I put together using
Canva's free service (https://canva.com).

What should you include in a Media Kit?

- **Short bio:** Introduce your channel and what topic area you cover on your channel.

- **Head shot:** Assuming you have a regular presence on your channel, include a close-up headshot of yourself, as brands generally prefer to work with personality based influencers. Alternatively, you can include a picture of your channel's logo.

- **Channel's reach:** Include the important metrics that brands like to see, subscriber count, monthly impressions, average views per video, how many comments or engagements you get per video. If your channel is still small or relatively new, focus on your channel's percentage growth each month, since you first created your channel.

- **Who your audience is:** Arguably the most important section is demonstrating that your viewers align well with the brand's target audience. This can be a screenshot of your YouTube analytics page showing a breakdown of your audience's age, gender and top geographical locations.

- **Social media reach:** Do not forget to also include your follower counts from any other social media platforms that you have an active presence on.

- **Sponsorship options:** This is where you include options for brands to collaborate with you. This can range from social media posts, hosting branded giveaways, an integration into one of your videos, a full dedicated video or even all of the above.

- **Sponsorship Testimonials:** If you have collaborated with any brands previously you could include screenshot examples of how you integrated their product and how your audience engaged with the brand.

- **Contact:** Be sure to add your business email or phone number at the end of the document so the brand can contact you to discuss pricing.

The ideal media kit should be prepared in a 1-2 page PDF document. Make it quick and easy for brands to see what you are all about. I have seen some media kits come in a 20-page PowerPoint presentation - unless a brand has specifically asked for a detailed proposal, this is a complete overkill. Be concise, and describe the ways you can benefit brands through exposure to your audience and include examples of how you could integrate brands within your content. Remember, the quality of your media kit represents the quality of your work, so make sure it represents your personal brand and channel well and get second opinions from friends or family before sending it out.

Make Yourself Easy To Reach

The first step to increasing your chances of landing a brand deal is to make yourself reachable. After spending time working at an influencer agency myself, I was surprised to see how difficult some influencers make it to contact them! Sometimes I had to spend 10 minutes digging through an influencer's website, merchandise store and social media pages to find a reliable way of contacting them. If you do not make yourself easy to reach you will miss out on potential opportunities.

At the very least make sure you have your contact email listed on the 'About' section on your YouTube channel. YouTube has a specific section on the 'About' page to add a business email that forces everyone to pass a reCAPTCHA (a test to tell human and bots apart) before they can access your email to cut down on spam. Some creators even go as far as adding their email to every video description, in case any potential advertisers stumble across one video and want to get in touch. Having your contact email listed on every social media platform you have a presence on will give you the best possible chance to be contacted. If a brand discovers your Instagram page for example - you cannot always assume they will take the time to search other social media platforms in order to contact you.

I would recommend creating two email addresses to manage your business opportunities. One email address that is listing publicly and another hidden email address that you can forward potential opportunities to from your public inbox. You are likely to receive a high volume of low quality emails to your public email address that do not warrant any reply from yourself. By separating your valuable contacts and leads to another inbox and replying from a private email - you will be able to respond faster and not miss out on any opportunities that would otherwise be lost in your public inbox.

Reaching Out To Brands

While you can sit back and wait for in-bound brand deals, the majority of my branded collaborations have actually originated from my own reach outs. I find many new creators are anxious about reaching out to brands, as they feel they are not large enough, or are scared of being declined. However, you never know what opportunities exist until you try - so you are likely missing out on deals by *not* reaching out!

Many brands have a quarterly marketing budget and love working with influencers. By reaching out you are showing that you actively have an interest in their products, and this saves them having to do the work seeking out influencers themselves.

Find brands and products that align well with your personality, content format and your channel's brand. If you have a niche gaming channel your audience is probably not interested in seeing a review of the latest Dyson Vacuum Cleaner.

Gaming channels in particular have an ever evolving industry of developers and publishers who are well versed in influencer marketing. For example, new indie developers who might not have any marketing budget, but are always willing to hand out free games to even the smallest influencers interested in covering their games.

If your channel is more niche focused, you may have to be a little more selective with your reach outs. Be creative with your proposals - what would you do with the product that would reflect positively on the brand?

Do not be demotivated if you feel like your messages are falling on deaf ears - my reach-outs are generally declined more often than they are accepted, and that is normal. Companies may be too busy to respond to requests at that time, have no marketing budget left for that quarter, or simply feel your channel does not align with their brand. Set yourself a goal to routinely reach out to several different brands every week. If a brand does respond to your request (even if it is a *"no"*), be sure to always thank them for their time and they may keep you in mind for a future opportunity.

Here is a template example for how a music creator might reach out to an equipment manufacturer.

E-mail Subject: **"YouTube Partnership Opportunity"**

> Dear ***company name***,
>
> I run a music-based YouTube channel with an audience of ***insert follower count*** and would love to discuss a potential partnership with your brand.
>
> I am already familiar with several of your products such as your bluetooth speakers and noise cancelling headphones that I regularly use in my studio. My audience primarily consists of music fans and producers and I believe they would be highly interested in your products.
>
> If this email has been sent to the wrong department, please forward this to the relevant marketing department.
>
> Best Regards,
>
> ***your name***

When it comes to requesting free video games. Here is a simple template I like to follow.

> Dear *company name*,
>
> I run a gaming YouTube channel with an audience of *insert follower count* and I upload on a weekly basis.
>
> I am highly interested in covering your game *insert game name*. Would you be willing to provide a game key and perhaps a few extra to get my audience involved?
>
> Best Regards,
>
> *your name*

PRICING YOUR CHANNEL

Sometimes a brand will offer you a price, but at other times they may ask you to come up with a number, or what your price or rate is! As a creator you need to be mindful not to over-charge and risk losing an opportunity - nor under-charge, leaving money on the table.

"How much should I charge?" is a common question among creators. Pricing in Influencer Marketing can be very arbitrary and subjective. There is no "going rate" as there are so many different variables and factors to consider that can influence the value of a sponsorship. Since each creator has a unique voice and audience, careful consideration must be taken with each opportunity.

I have managed influencer sponsorships with both large and small creators, and have seen a broad spectrum of payment rates. A good starting point is to work out your average view count. Take the last 10 videos you have uploaded, and calculate the average number of views per video to estimate your average viewership.

Generally, a branded video tends to sit around the $0.04 CPV (Cost Per View) mark. You can use this formula to estimate how much you can expect to receive given your viewership.

$$\text{Sponsorship Rate} = \textit{Average Viewership} \times \textit{CPV}$$

If you estimate your average viewership to be 10,000 views per video. With a $0.04 CPV, you could request a payment of $400.

Negotiating Payments:

I have seen the rate for sponsored videos vary from $0.01 - $0.10 CPV - depending on the brand and influencers involved. Many brands will assign a price based only on average views as a benchmark. However pricing on average views alone does not take other factors, such as engagement, into consideration, so this can be your leverage in a negotiation.

Use **discretion** when it comes to sponsorships. I accepted a very low paying sponsorship (around the $0.01 CPV range), as it involved promoting a video game I was already posting regularly on my channel - so it aligned perfectly with my content. However, there have been brands or products I enjoy, but do not necessarily fit within my channel's theme - so I tend to charge more.

Here are some factors that you can use when negotiating your payment:

* **Integration Type:** Dedicated branded videos tend to offer a higher CPV - however they can be more intrusive for your audience. Many times I have negotiated with a brand to 'integrate' their product within one of my normal videos rather than creating a dedicated video for the product. Although this sometimes results in a lower payment than a fully dedicated video, it is worth it, because my audiences may respond more positively to a less

invasive promotion. Integrating a brand into a normal video can also result in the video receiving *more* views than if it was a dedicated brand video, as viewers can be less likely to click on a video that seems out of the ordinary.

- **Niche Content:** If your channel is creating content around a niche that a brand specifically wants to target, this can give you *huge* leverage in a negotiation. For example, if you create content around horses, a brand selling horse care products may be willing to pay a much higher CPV to target a dedicated audience who are more likely to be consumers of their product.

- **Production Costs:** If the video will take longer than normal to create or require extra production costs to film, you should factor this into your fee.

- **Social Media Amplification:** In addition to your branded video, adding coverage to your social media pages can reach more of your audience and help increase the brand's budget for your collaboration.

- **Usage Period:** If a brand wants to use the sponsored content you created for their own social media platforms, this is usually outlined in a 'usage period' such as 6 months, and can warrant an additional talent fee.

- **Exclusivity:** If the agreement requires that you do not work with any competitors for a defined period of time, this can result in you having to walk away from other potential deals and may warrant an additional fee.

- **No Ads:** Sometimes brands will require that the sponsored YouTube video is uploaded unmonetised (ad revenue turned off) to prevent any competitor's products being shown. Since this will result in the uploaded video earning no advertising revenue, this could be used as a reason to quote a higher fee.

PROHIBITED ADVERTISEMENTS

Before committing to a commercial relationship with a brand, always check it adheres to Google's Ad Policy[17]. These guidelines outline prohibited products and content formats.

A disallowed sponsored content format is 'burned in' ads. A burned in ad is where an advertiser provides their own commercial for you to insert into your content. While advertisers are allowed to provide assets to showcase within a sponsored video, this should be edited and presented to your audience with your message.

Google also restrict certain kinds of businesses from advertising to prevent users from being exploited. Google's Ad Policy also covers industries and products that have specific restrictions in place, such as adult content, alcohol, gambling and games of chance, healthcare, tobacco and misleading products to name a few. If a product sounds too good to be true, it is better to err on the side of caution - otherwise your video may be removed, and in some cases your channel being removed from the YouTube Partner Program.

DISCLOSURES

It is good practice to be transparent with your audience when a brand has sponsored an integration in your video. Trying to hide a sponsorship will not only damage the trust of your audience if they find out, but may result in legal consequences if you do not abide by disclosure obligations.

YouTube also requires any paid product placements or endorsements to be marked on the video's settings. This allows YouTube to adjust the ads they run to prevent any potential conflicts with brand partners.

---

17   https://support.google.com/youtube/answer/154235

This may also impact the CPM that your video will generate, as well as where the video is surfaced on YouTube.

How to mark paid sponsorships:

1. Sign into YouTube and visit your creator studio (https://studio. youtube.com)

2. Select Edit next to the appropriate video

3. Select the Advanced tab

4. Check the box that states "This video contains paid promotion such as paid product placement, sponsorships or endorsement"

Depending what country you reside in, you will have different disclosure requirements for paid promotions. In Britain, the Advertising Standards Authority (https://www.asa.org.uk) have set guidelines for influencers and social media marketers. If you reside in the United States you will need to follow endorsement guidelines outlined by The Federal Trade Commission (https://www.ftc.gov).

BEST PRACTICES:

- **Be selective**: When brands first started contacting me I was so excited I wanted to work with everyone! It is ok to say "no" to a sponsorship - especially if you feel like the brand or product is not a good fit for your channel or audience. For instance, a website that facilitates online gambling might offer a great payment - but is it the best fit for your audience? It may also violate Google's Ad Policy!

- **Communicate Expectations**: If you are uncomfortable with a stipulation or deliverable from a brand, it is always best to be upfront. The best partnerships have clear expectations, so both the creator and brand know exactly what to expect from the end result. It is always better to *over*-deliver than *under*-deliver.

- **Be honest with your fans**: Being transparent with your audience is important, especially when a payment is involved. If you promote a bad product, this can break the trust of your audience and reflect badly on your channel.

- **Space out your brand deals**: Your audience may grow tired if every video you upload contains branded content. Allow for sufficient breathing room between sponsored content.

- **Involve your viewers**: Asking a brand if they can provide extra units to giveaway is a great way to increase engagement on the branded video and get your audience to interact with the product.

- **Read your contract**: It is vital that you read and understand the legal agreement. Have a family member, or even a lawyer review the contract *before* you sign it. Take note of the deliverables, payment terms and due dates of drafts.

- **Professionalism**: Being polite and professional goes a long way when dealing with brands. I have seen cases where unprofessional or demanding influencers (or in some cases agents acting on behalf of an influencer), have been blacklisted from future deals. Having a positive experience with a brand can lead to more future opportunities.

CHAPTER 5 CHECKLIST

Making money from YouTube is important for sustainability. As your channel grows and demands more from you, monetisation will provide an income to allow you to focus on the channel full-time, and even hire a team to help you!

Follow this checklist to monetise your channel to its full potential.

☐ *Join the YouTube Partnership Program*

☐ *Follow YouTube's Advertiser Friendly Guidelines for the best ad rates*

☐ *Create Merchandise relevant to your audience*

☐ *Allow your fans to support you with crowdfunding*

☐ *Always use affiliate links when promoting products*

☐ *Create a Media Kit*

☐ *Do your own reach-outs to brands you want to work with*

TOOLS AND RESOURCES

There are many tools and third party resources to help take your channel to the next level. Ranging from tools to assist social media growth, marketplaces to find designers, and music to use in monetized videos. Here is a collection of the best resources I have found for YouTubers.

GROWTH TOOLS

Google Trends (https://trends.google.com/trends/)

This is an official website by Google that analyses the interest in given keywords. You can compare search volume, over time, between different terms and use this to determine which keywords you should prioritize when optimising your videos.

SOCIAL NETWORKING

Bitly (http://bitly.com)

A free service that allows you to shorten URLs and create a custom link that never expires. For example, you can create a link to re-direct straight to your channel with *bit.ly/yourchannelname*. The website also provides useful statistics showing total clicks, referrers and location.

ClicktoTweet (http://clicktotweet.com)

You can create a predefined tweet that viewers can share with one click. If a viewer clicks on your link they will have your message inserted into their Twitter status box ready to be shared. You can also use this tool to track the analytics and demographics of your link over time.

Meetup (http://meetup.com)

Discover local meetups and communities of like-minded creators.

MARKETING

Canva (https://canva.com)

Easily create a professional looking Media Kit design using Canva's drag and drop feature. Even the free version includes a huge variety of templates, images and shapes to create a great design.

Gleam (http://gleam.io)

Hosting giveaways is a breeze with Gleam. You can create a professional looking landing page where viewers can enter into a giveaway with their social platforms and actively earn entries by following your chosen social media pages. Try teaming up with brands or other creators to collaboratively promote a giveaway that will cross-pollinate your audiences.

Mailchimp (http://mailchimp.com)

With MailChimp you can grow an email list of viewers and send out professional looking emails. You could use this to promote your new awesome t-shirt on sale, or just let your viewers know about your latest upload.

VistaPrint (https://www.vistaprint.com)

Create custom business cards, fliers, brochures, and even pop-up banners at a very affordable price. If you are attending any networking events, this website is a must.

CREATIVE PRODUCTION

Fiverr (http://fiverr.com)

Fiverr is an online marketplace where you can purchase freelance services that start as cheap as $5. You can purchase all kinds of services ranging from graphics and design, voice over actors, and even virtual assistants. Of course the quality depends on how much you are willing to spend, but if you are looking for a quick, low cost logo this could be a good first stop.

If you want to use my referral link, you can get 20% off your first order (http://bit.ly/fiverrdiscount)

RIOT (http://luci.criosweb.ro/riot)

Radical Image Optimisation Tool (RIOT) is a free image optimizer that will allow you to visually adjust compression parameters to reduce the file size of an image. This is useful to reduce thumbnails under the 2MB size limit without sacrificing too much image quality.

Picmaker (https://www.picmaker.io)

Free, fast and easy to use YouTube Thumbnail creator. Step up your thumbnail game by adding high quality text, sticker effects and a large selection of eye attracting thumbnail backgrounds.

ANALYTICS

Socialblade (http://socialblade.com)

Socialblade is a great resource to have bookmarked. You can enter any YouTube username and see the historical growth statistics for that channel. It will break down the daily, monthly and yearly video views, subscribers and estimated earnings.

VidIQ (http://vidiq.com)

VidIQ offers a free browser extension that displays additional stats next to any video watch page. This is helpful to evaluate how other videos are ranking, where they are being discovered, and also how you can optimise your own content. My favourite part about this extension is that it shows what tags other YouTube creators use - and how high their video is ranking on that search term.

MONETISATION

Amazon Affiliates (https://affiliate-program.amazon.com)

Whenever you link to a product on Amazon, you should be using an Affiliate link to earn commission when viewers purchase a product you promote. It is free to join and you can earn up to 10% advertising fees by just recommending products you use.

Famebit (http://famebit.com)

Famebit is a self-service platform connecting influencers to brands. In 2016 Famebit was acquired by Google. As a creator you can link your YouTube channel and social media pages to the platform and submit proposals to current brand opportunities on the platform. Once you are registered with Famebit your channel will be visible to brands using the platform which they can use to find influencers to promote their products

Patreon (http://patreon.com)

If your channel is not eligible for YouTube Channel Memberships, Patreon is the next best thing. Your most dedicated fans can choose to support your channel through monthly donations providing a sustainable income stream.

MUSIC RESOURCES

Audio library (https://www.youtube.com/audiolibrary/music)

YouTube has its own ever-growing Audio Library offering a huge collection of free sound effects and music that can be monetised on the platform! The music can be streamed and downloaded in high quality 320kbp MP3. Be sure to check for music marked as *'attribution-required'* - this means you should credit the artist in the video description.

Monstercat (https://www.monstercat.com/licensing/content-creators)

If you like Electronic music then you will love Monstercat. They have a special program for content creators offering a whitelist of their music - this protects you from YouTube's content ID and allows you to keep 100% of the advertising revenue your video makes.

EQUIPMENT AND SOFTWARE

A common question for new creators is *'what equipment do I need?'*. I have compiled a list of all the video equipment I would recommend to start a YouTube channel.

Keep in mind that content is still king – no matter how expensive your equipment, you will still need a solid content strategy to back it up and to grow your channel.

I have also created an Amazon storefront to list all the equipment I currently use to create my videos.

USA: https://www.amazon.com/shop/silentc0re

UK: https://www.amazon.co.uk/shop/silentc0re

GAMEPLAY

If you are a PC gamer, gameplay footage can be easily captured straight from your computer. There is a fantastic free program that allows both video recording and live streaming called Open Broadcaster Software (https://obsproject.com/)

If you are recording from a mobile device or console, a capture card is a must. It is a small device that connects between your game console and computer. Elgato (https://www.elgato.com) offers one of the best in the market and I have used their capture cards for over 5 years. Currently I use the Elgato Game Capture Card HD60 S, that allows streaming and recording in 1080p and 60 frames per second.

AUDIO

A good microphone should be one of your first priorities. The Blue Snowball is a great starter microphone - it plugs right into your computer using a USB and has a great quality sound. If you have a little more budget available, I would recommend going for the Blue Yeti USB Microphone (this is what I use). It has more options available on the microphone as well as four different recording modes to adjust to your setup. If you order directly from Bluedesigns (https://www.bluedesigns.com/), you can use 'silent' as a promo code to save 20%.

You may also find a boom arm handy for recording audio. A boom arm clamps onto your desk and suspends your microphone in place, allowing you to speak into it directly. I would also recommend using a boom arm with a swivel so you can easily move the microphone for recording, and then tuck it away when you are finished.

To record the audio to my computer I use a program called Audacity (https://www.audacityteam.org). It is easy to use, allows for multi-track audio editing and is absolutely free!

VIDEO

Most smartphones have cameras offering adequate video quality. Just remember to always hold your phone horizontally to best fit YouTube's video player.

Logitech offers some great webcam options that record in 1080p quality – some of them even offer background replacement technology specifically for YouTube.

When it comes to purchasing a professional camera – there is no 'best option'. The options vary dramatically based on usage and budget. There are three main types of cameras to consider - compact, mirrorless and DSLR.

If I had to choose one camera to use for vlogging, I would choose the Canon Powershot G7X. It is a 20.2 megapixel pocketable camera, with a front facing LCD touch panel and a reasonable price point. I would recommend doing your own research to find the best option for your needs before purchasing a camera.

LIGHTING

Although not a requirement, good lighting can make you look much more flattering on camera! Sunlight is a great source of lighting that is absolutely free, try shooting your videos while facing a window to make use of natural daylight.

For more advanced setups, you can use a two-point or three-point lighting system. In my videos I use a single Ring Light facing me directly, with my camera fixed into the center mount.

GLOSSARY

Here is a collection of important words to help you understand the terminology on and around YouTube.

» **Ad (#AD)**: This is commonly used to mark that a video has been sponsored

» **AMA**: Ask me Anything - Similar to a Q&A however usually indicates the questions can be asked with no limits

» **ASMR**: Autonomous Sensory Meridian Response - Videos are tagged by this if they trigger a tingling sensation by the creator whispering or softly speaking into a microphone

» **Block Shooting**: Recording multiple videos in one sitting

» **CPM**: Cost Per Mille - The average amount of advertising revenue generated for each thousand views

» **Call to Action (CTA)**: Action taken by viewers on a clickable button such as 'Like' or 'Subscribe'

» **CTR**: Click-through rate. The percentage of viewers that clicked to view your video after being exposed to it

» **CPC**: Cost per Click - When a brand offers a specific payment per user that clicks a tracked URL

» **CPI**: Cost per Install - When a brand offers a specific payment per user that installs an app or software through a tracked URL

» **CPD**: Cost per Download - When a brand offers a specific payment per user that downloads an app or software through a tracked URL

» **CPV**: Cost per view - When a brand offers a specific payment per view on a specific video

» **DITL**: Day In The Life - where creators offer an insight into their daily routine

» **Content ID:** Videos can receive a content ID claim if they contain any copyright-protected material such as music or TV shows

» **Demographics**: This is a breakdown of your subscribers such as age, gender and geographical location

» **End-Slate**: An end slate is a standard outro that will display branded graphics and prompts to subscribe or visit another video

» **Embedded Videos**: When a video is integrated into a website so it can be viewed on another page instead of YouTube

» **GRWM**: Get Ready With Me - When a creator shares their morning routine

» **Haul**: A popular term with lifestyle influencers, this is a video discussing items that have been purchased

» **Impression**: When viewers are exposed to your video thumbnail, even if they do not click to view the video

» **Interactions**: An interaction is counted when a viewer likes, dislikes or leave a comment on your video

» **OOTD**: Showcasing your Outfit Of The Day

» **Media Kit**: A document containing information about your channel that can be provided to brands or journalists

» **Metadata**: Your video title, description and tags is all considered metadata and will be used by YouTube to rank your content

» **SEO**: Search Engine Optimisation - This makes it easier for YouTube and Google to understand your video and rank it for the appropriate audience

» **Shoutout**: A shoutout is generally a verbal mention to a person or channel

» **Optimisation**: Optimising your channel will improve all the best elements

» **Q&A**: Question and Answer. Often creators will offer their audience an opportunity to ask questions

» **ROI**: Return on Investment - A measure of the rates of return on money invested in order to decide whether or not to undertake an investment

» **Unique viewers**: An estimate of the amount of *different* people who view your videos. This number shows ultimately how big your audience is.

» **View**s: A user will have to watch around 30 seconds of your video for it to be counted as a view on YouTube

» **Watermark**: A branded watermark will appear on all your videos and is usually your channel's logo

ACKNOWLEDGEMENTS

Writing a book turned out to be a much harder (and longer) process than I could ever imagine! While I can turn around a video in a few hours, writing a book was the best part of 2 years of work.

I have to start by thanking YouTube for creating a platform allowing me to express myself from the comfort of my own bedroom, build confidence in my abilities, and help fuel a new career at a point when I felt very unsure what I wanted to do with my life.

Secondly, thank you to my amazing audience who have watched and supported me on YouTube! 10 years later, I am still inspired to create content because of the amazing community that YouTube is comprised of.

A special thank you to Stuart Harper for keeping my grammar in check, and my family for their unconditional support since the very beginning.